PRAISE FOR *UNRIVALED*

"Are you falling into fatal traps that derail your brand's potential? Do you wonder whether and why you even need a brand, or doubt how a strong brand can deliver economic power and help you grow? Does your brand hint at a one-size-fits-all, rinse-and-repeat philosophy, or is it tailored to laser-focused insights about your customer—the whole customer and the full context of how your brand fits into their lives? If these questions are making you hesitate, it's time to leverage Michelle's deep experience advancing start-ups and established companies alike to create a new playbook for go-to-market success. Get under the hood of the holy grail of high-growth brand strategy and read this book."

—SUSAN FOURNIER
professor and dean, Boston University
Questrom School of Business

"*Unrivaled* is the ultimate customer-centered growth playbook. The framework breaks down what it takes to earn the top spot— and stay there. It's a must-read for anyone tired of being locked in tight competition and ready to play a different game. As Michelle would say, 'Giddy up!'"

—KATHERINE OTWAY
chief marketing officer, The Engine

"*Unrivaled* is an outstanding read. Heath's practical and relatable storytelling ability kept me locked in all the way. Her five-step framework is clear and compelling. It focuses on being intentional and prescriptive in both strategy and execution. If you are looking for a way to drive growth in your business, this book isn't optional . . . it's a must."

—JERRY PATTERSON
head of advanced wealth solutions, Cetera Financial Group

"In *Unrivaled*, Michelle Heath unveils the secret to unstoppable growth: relentless customer obsession. Her bold, practical framework transforms businesses into brands customers can't live without—essential reading for organizations ready to put the customer at the heart of growth to dominate their market."

—DIANE HESSAN
award-winning entrepreneur, innovator,
and author of *Customer-Centered Growth*

"For over a decade, I've been listening to Michelle as she works with her clients. Banking, tech, luxury, cybersecurity, construction—you name the industry, she gets it. If you're tired of throwing random arrows trying to hit the bullseye, just read *Unrivaled*. She has all the answers!"

—GARY FLEMING
chief executive officer of Winter Sports Retailers, Inc.,
and Michelle's husband

"This book is for bold builders and growth go-getters. *Unrivaled* is the secret weapon to create your bullseye vision, unlock your unique potential, and go to market with unrivaled 'surround sound' to stand alone at number one."

—SUE BURTON KIRDAHY
senior vice president, member experience,
Digital Federal Credit Union

"Hypori was seeking a succinct way to communicate our technology to the market in a new and uncluttered way. This required a completely different view of our tone and tenor to the market, graphics and illustrations, and descriptive ways of defining and projecting our use cases to our key verticals. The Unrivaled Growth Framework™ uncovered our 'secret sauce' and aligned the entire organization with what matters most to our customers. I firmly believe this critical work is foundational to our accelerated growth in the market!"

—WAYNE LEWANDOWSKI
chief revenue officer, Hypori

"In *Unrivaled*, Michelle Heath brilliantly reframes how we think about brand—not as a static identity but as a dynamic, customer-first growth engine. This book challenges leaders to rethink the role of their brand, shifting from a supporting player to the driving force behind competitive growth. Michelle's approach is bold, actionable, and deeply aligned with the power of reframing: seeing opportunities differently to create transformative outcomes. For anyone ready to elevate their brand and outpace the competition, *Unrivaled* is the ultimate guide."

—MONA PATEL
transformative growth mindset coach, author of *Reframe*,
and creator of the Nine-Minute Reframe process

"*Unrivaled* is a master class in transforming business growth by unlocking the customer mindset. Michelle offers readers a powerful road map to differentiate, adapt, and achieve sustained excellence with an absolute focus on the customer, which is where she thrives. The framework and insights are not just theoretical—they are practical and actionable tools that can be immediately put to work to drive results. This book is essential reading for anyone who aims to innovate and execute at the highest level."

—JOHN MATOS
digital transformation leader and
customer engagement visionary

"*Unrivaled* is a must-read for anyone aiming to transform their business into a market leader. Through her proprietary Unrivaled Growth Framework™, Michelle provides actionable insights for standing out in crowded markets, building emotional connections with customers, and creating sustainable growth. Her approach as a marketing maverick shines throughout the book, offering a fresh perspective on aligning business ethos, customer obsession, and innovative strategies. This book is not just a guide but a call to action for businesses ready to leave the competition in the rearview mirror!"

—JOHN SHORT
chief executive officer, Compound Growth Marketing

UNRIVALED

amplify
an imprint of Amplify Publishing Group

www.amplifypublishinggroup.com

Unrivaled: Five Steps to Achieving Explosive Business Growth

For more information, please contact:
Amplify Publishing, an imprint of Amplify Publishing Group
620 Herndon Parkway, Suite 220
Herndon, VA 20170
info@amplifypublishing.com

Library of Congress Control Number: 2024917078

CPSIA Code: PRV0325A

ISBN-13: 979-8-89138-372-2

Printed in the United States

*For my father, Robert A. Abair, aka Pop, Gramps, Bob,
and Bobby, whose advice, encouragement, and
inspiration have made all the difference in my life.
You are Unrivaled.*

*In loving memory of Doris O. (Abair) Paolini
August 25, 1920–March 6, 2023
To my grandmother, our "Mémère," and the life of the
party, who constantly reminded me that every day is
a gift and inspired me to keep writing and follow this
dream. In the words of her beloved Perry Como,
"And I Love You So."*

UNRIVALED

Five Steps to Achieving Explosive Business Growth

MICHELLE HEATH

FOUNDER & CEO, GROWTH STREET

amplify

an imprint of Amplify Publishing Group

CONTENTS

STEP 1: OBSESS

STEP 2: DIFFERENTIATE

STEP 3: COMMIT

STEP 4: EXECUTE

STEP 5: ADAPT

PREFACE

"The meaning of life is to find your gift.
The purpose of life is to give it away."
—**PABLO PICASSO**

I had settled into a cozy booth at a bustling lunch spot in Boston. A long-time friend and colleague was sitting across from me. We were sharing all the life updates—our kids, spouses, work, mutual connections—when I blurted out, "I'm writing a book." I could see him thoughtfully forming his response as he took a bite of his lunch. He replied, "A book. Interesting. Why?"

His response caught me off guard. I was early in writing this manuscript. I had just started to "say it out loud," which made it feel more real. Most people replied to my book-writing declaration with: "Wow, that's amazing!" or "Good for you!" I wasn't expecting the question *why*—I am always so prepared, yet I did not have a response ready. After what seemed like an eternity of him waiting and me thinking, I answered his question. "I'm writing this book to share what I know with the world. I want to help every CEO and executive think differently about business growth and show them a new way to do it. I want to share my gifts to help other people. I want everyone to know what I know."

It was at that moment that I knew I needed to write this book.

I talk about business growth as a winding road that's full of lots of twists and turns, potholes and dead ends, speed bumps and detours. Like when we miss a turn and the GPS is "recalculating"—during this writing journey, there have been many moments where I was trying to figure out the path forward.

When I founded my business, Growth Street, in 2013, it was to take the road less traveled. After decades as a successful business leader and operator for Fortune 500 and start-up companies, I was on a new adventure.

My first client was a bootstrapped start-up. The CEO called me in because she needed some executive marketing horsepower to reach the company's aggressive business goals. I rolled up my sleeves with her team and built marketing campaigns that doubled the pipeline, delivered $100,000 of revenue, and increased the average order value, all within a few short months.

Fast-forward ten-plus years and I have been under the hoods of businesses across just about every industry—from fashion to financial services, cybersecurity to construction, blockchain to the built world, and health care to HR tech. I have put my Unrivaled Growth Framework to work with over fifty companies and hundreds of business leaders. I helped a biotech company go from $25 billion to $50 billion by optimizing ten to fifteen acquisitions a year. I have worked with family-owned, VC-backed, and PE-backed companies, all at different growth stages, all with aggressive growth goals. Together with my clients, we've built Unrivaled brands, resulting in more than $100 billion in revenue growth, and that number keeps climbing.

As I was working with my clients, I realized I had the itch to start writing a book. It started with a germ of an idea about the power of building an emotional connection between brands and people. I started writing and stopped. Internal doubt and fear crept in. I thought, "Does the world need my ideas? What do I possibly know about writing a book?" I shuttered the draft away in a folder on my hard drive.

But the seed had been planted and kept calling me back. A few years later, I dusted off the draft chapters and realized my thinking had evolved. The initial ideas were still part of the story, but they weren't the entire story. The story I wanted to tell was bigger and it was clearer. I began tying together all of the work I had done for my clients to help them fix nagging growth problems, turn around business results, and achieve audacious company goals. I looked for patterns and trends across all of the companies I had led growth for as an in-house CMO and growth executive. I started taking what was in my head—my secret-sauce process—and sketching it out on paper as a framework. I started, stopped, and started over. The road eventually led me here: to *Unrivaled*.

For all the leaders, founders, thinkers, doers, visionaries, operators, innovators, entrepreneurs, investors, creators, learners, teachers, builders, dreamers—this book is for you. I am so excited to share what I know to help you think differently about how to grow your business.

I give you the power to be Unrivaled. Now, let's . . . ***Giddy Up!***

LIPSTICK ON A PIG

"In a crowded marketplace, fitting in is failing. In a busy marketplace, not standing out is the same as being invisible."
—SETH GODIN, FROM HIS BESTSELLING BOOK,
PURPLE COW

My phone rang early on a Monday morning. After quick introductions, the CEO told me why he was calling.

"I need a new logo," he said emphatically.

"Why?" I asked curiously.

"I need my business to stand out. I'll tell you more when we meet," he said hastily.

A few days later, I was sitting in the executive boardroom, waiting for him to enter.

Quick sidenote: What you need to know about what I do is that most of the time, I have no idea what I'm walking into. I might have a few clues from a phone conversation, an email volley, or a warm referral, but typically I'm going in cold. Every business is different, requiring me to quickly catalog all of the situations I've encountered and rapidly surface solutions. It is why I love what I do. And now, back to the story.

The CEO came in and sat across the table from me.

I asked him to tell me about the company—what was working, what wasn't, the business economics, today's customers versus his ideal customers—all questions to get the wheels turning.

He told me the company, a family-owned and family-run business, was approaching $1 billion in revenue, and he wanted a way to close the gap on the competition to get there faster. He was riled up about the competitive landscape and told me that he was seeing the competition at every turn. He said his main competitors were winning more deals—both new and repeat business—and he thought a new logo would help him compete.

If I had a dollar for every new business meeting that started with "We need a new logo."

Reality check: A new logo might make your business look different, but it won't solve your growth problem. First of all, "different" is highly subjective. I love purple and you love blue. I love sans-serif fonts and you love serif fonts. Secondly, what I like and what you like does not matter. What matters is what your customers like. What resonates with them? What connects you to them? What immediately grabs their attention? *What is the competitive advantage your company has in the eyes of your customers?*

My new client wanted to revitalize his business and ignite growth so powerful it became unstoppable. Great goal. But growth doesn't come from a new logo; it comes from inside the heart of your business. I asked, "Why do you think you need a new logo?"

He answered without pause, "Because we are losing some big contracts to our largest competitors, and we're not winning repeat contracts from existing customers. Plus, I am seeing our top competitors everywhere, and they are really pushing their brand. So I was thinking that a new logo would help us win more deals."

I could tell we needed to take this conversation in a different direction.

I parked the logo discussion with the CEO and started asking more questions about his business. We talked about their go-to-market strategy, revenue targets, pipeline trends, and competition—and I spent time turning over all the rocks. As I listened, the theme of "repeat business" kept coming up. I followed the thread and asked, "Tell me more about new versus repeat business—what percentage of business would you say is new, and what percentage is repeat?"

He paused for a while to think. He picked his head up and said, "Being really honest, I don't know. If I were to guess, I would say we're really good at closing the first deal, but I'd say only about 25 percent of revenue is from repeat business. Might be even less. I know our existing customers are going out to bid on contracts, and we're not winning them."

I had to tell my client that a logo was not going to fix his problem. A new logo would simply be, to borrow a phrase, like putting lipstick on a pig. Pretty on the outside, but not any better beneath the surface. To plug the hole that was draining away repeat business, to beat out his competition at every turn, and to achieve his aggressive revenue goal faster—he needed a different solution. Like many businesses I've worked with over the past thirty years, this CEO knew where he wanted to go, but he needed new tools to get there.

Fortunately, I knew I could help him. My company is called Growth Street, and I've spent nearly three decades helping businesses unlock explosive growth. Together, we've built Unrivaled brands with our clients, resulting in more than $100 billion in revenue growth, using a system that is so efficient, so effective, and so powerful, it propels companies to explosive growth and Unrivaled market leadership. I call this proprietary approach the **Unrivaled Growth Framework**.

As I tell all my clients, once you put this five-step framework into action, ROI soars, customers become loyal fans, and your team is mobilized and motivated. Strategic decisions become easy and clear. You become the Unrivaled leader in your market.

I turned to the CEO and smiled as I rolled up my sleeves. ***"Giddy Up!"***

CHAPTER 1

GOOD TO GREAT TO GONE: THE SIX MISTAKES SUCCESSFUL BUSINESSES MAKE

"If I had to live my life again,
I'd make the same mistakes, only sooner."

—TALLULAH BANKHEAD, AWARD-WINNING
ACTRESS AND POLITICAL ACTIVIST

One of the most famous business books of all time is Jim Collins's *Good to Great*. I remember my boss gave me a copy as I was taking on my first leadership role and climbing the executive ladder. I read it cover to cover, carefully taking notes in the margins and soaking in the concepts.

The book has become almost a rite of passage for executives and entrepreneurs—the blueprint for building a great company. What many people don't realize, however, is that a number of the companies Collins profiled eventually crashed and burned, got sold off, or are now a shadow of the successful enterprises they were when he wrote the book. Remember Circuit City? Bankrupt and now trying to claw its way back. Wells Fargo? A dumpster fire, lurching from scandal to scandal. Gillette? Sold to Procter & Gamble and then hammered by two upstart competitors, Dollar Shave Club and Harry's.

What went wrong? To put it simply, the leaders of those once-great enterprises took their eyes off the ball. You've probably heard of many of these companies. They were once **Unrivaled**. They had the market leader position—the competitive advantage, the tailwind for efficient growth, the power play. But they lost it.

Even great companies can fall victim to fatal mistakes. Mistakes that drain precious cash flow, suck up time, and erode morale. Mistakes that get in the way of gaining economies of scale and achieving ambitious revenue goals. Mistakes that take you off the road to Unrivaled and speeding instead into a dead end. I don't want you to make the same mistakes.

Over the years, I've found that these "dead-end mistakes" fall into six categories—all of which are extremely common, might even sound familiar, and are easily avoidable.

You might be tempted to skim over the mistakes because they feel uncomfortable. Maybe you're thinking, "I would never make a mistake like this!" Set your assumptions and preconceptions aside.

Open your mind.

Take in a deep breath.

Hold on tight.

Here we go.

Mistake #1: The Echo Chamber

All too often, company growth stalls out because you're stuck in the **Echo Chamber**. Businesses become too inwardly focused—talking to themselves instead of living externally and listening to their customers. How do you know when you're in the Echo Chamber?

- When the only voices you hear are your own.

- When you don't know the customers' words and what they think, want, and expect.

- When your personal opinions and biases drive decisions.

- When you fail to live in the customer mindset.

These businesses become complacent and concentrate their attention inward, on the organization itself, rather than outward, on their customers and target market. It's like putting on a blindfold before racing into battle. You end up beat up, exhausted, and frustrated—or worse.

The Echo Chamber is an easy place to get trapped. In the blink of an eye, you're subsumed into the day-to-day—focusing your attention in the weeds—fixing operations, building technology, defining product features, aligning sales and marketing, and the list goes on. Sure, these are important aspects of running the business, but when your inward focus takes over, you lose touch with your customers. And that's when the competition sweeps in and eats your lunch.

Paradoxically, many internally focused companies waste an inordinate amount of time eyeballing their competition—trying to second-guess them, imitating what they do (or flat-out copying it) if it seems to work. On the surface, that looks like outward focus. But you can't copy your way to explosive growth.

I was consulting for a Fortune 500 financial services company. They were behind in their market and wanted to leapfrog the competition. Instead of looking at what prospects and customers needed and wanted, the CEO was completely obsessed with doing what the competition did at every turn: "Did you see what they put on their website today? We've got to change our website! Did you see they launched a new ad campaign? Call the agency—we need to rethink our ad campaigns! Did you see they unveiled a new product? Put a task force together to build one!" They wound up spending millions of dollars building a product because their competitor built one—not because their customer base wanted or needed one. Had they spent the time asking and listening to customers, they could have had a breakthrough moment and created a product or experience that connected with their customers and put them in a market leadership position. Instead, they wasted time and money on a copycat product. Rather than imitating your competition, you need to focus on your customers. Their needs, wants, desires—even the very words they use—should be your signposts. Customers are fickle and easily swayed to switch. If you're not engaging, relating, and connecting with them in meaningful ways all the time, they're gone.

When I am brought in to help a business, many times the executives believe they know the customer. They get reports on Net Promoter Score, call logs, and customer success trends. But most of the time, the executives do not *know* the customer—they do not live in the customer mindset. These well-intentioned executives might have been part of the sales cycle at one point in the business's life, but over time, business leaders can get too far away from the customer. When that happens, personal bias creeps in and informs decisions. Customers are constantly changing. The language and approach that attracted them years ago might not resonate anymore. If you're inwardly focused, you're going to pass right by your ideal customer. Getting out of sync with the customer is what happens when you're in the Echo Chamber.

Mistake #2: The Missing Business Ethos

"What do you want to be when you grow up?"

I bet each of us has been asked that question a hundred times. The search for what we want to be begins when we are young. My earliest memory of being asked that question was in the first grade. Sister Sandra had us all draw a picture of what we wanted to be. Some kids drew policemen or astronauts. I drew a picture of me as a veterinarian, surrounded by horses with a stethoscope around my neck. I don't have that drawing anymore (it could be living in my parents' attic), but I still remember how vividly what I wanted to be was in my mind. I was so passionate about my Vision it consumed me.

The search for who and what we want to be runs deep and drives us forward as people and as a society. Our personal values and dreams create an ethos that shapes the contribution we hope to make to the world and determines how we achieve our Vision.

When we start businesses and lead companies, we have the opportunity to ask: "What do we want our business to be when it grows up?" Whether you're building a business from scratch or leading a one-hundred-year-old company, knowing your business identity—why, who, and what you stand for—is essential to success.

When businesses fail to answer this question, they make the mistake of the **Missing Business Ethos**.

Think of Business Ethos as the soul of your business. It includes your North Star Vision for a better world. It encompasses the values, ethics, and purpose that guide your decisions. It defines your company's character, and when communicated to your target market, it creates an authentic emotional connection. Business Ethos is what you stand for so you can stand out to your ideal customer.

This idea of ethos was planted by the Greek philosopher Aristotle. For Aristotle, the purpose of a speaker's ethos was to "inspire trust in his audience." Ethos was how the speaker communicated with the audience and created a connection, and it was "achieved through the orator's 'good sense, good moral character, and goodwill.'"[1]

Staying true to your Business Ethos also inspires trust in your audience. For Unrivaled companies, the Business Ethos is evident in everything they do, giving their customers reasons to trust and believe—before, during, and after they buy—and giving employees, investors, partners, and shareholders a belief system that compels them to be dedicated to achieving the company's North Star Vision.

A Missing Business Ethos will almost certainly undermine performance, morale, and results. The mistake typically comes in two flavors:

1. **Set it and forget it:** Some businesses define their ethos early on but fail to actually live up to it or to consistently put their ethos into action. They may say the words, but their actions don't seem to match their stated values and purpose. Eventually they might say the right words, but they are just not "walking the talk."

2. **Forget to set it:** On the other hand, the number of businesses I come across that have never spent the time to create their ethos is too many to count. Founders and CEOs want to get moving, and ethos takes time and energy to define. But without a clearly defined Business Ethos, you are almost sure to lose your way.

Take Wells Fargo, for instance. They set it—and forgot it.

As one of the *Good to Great* companies, Wells Fargo's rise to greatness included over one hundred years of impressive business growth.[2]

When you read what Wells Fargo stands for, you see things like: "On March 18, 1852, our founders—Henry Wells and William G. Fargo—built an innovative start-up to help customers build businesses and manage money in a rapidly changing world. Their dedication to finding creative solutions and advocating for more inclusive communities continues to inspire generations of changemakers to build the history of what's next . . . for generations, we've been helping people go further. From exchanging gold coins for paper checks to enabling online transactions, we're continually innovating so our customers can get ahead."[3]

Would you believe in a company that said these things? If these values matter to you, not only would you believe, but you would also open an account, transfer your money, and trust them to do what they said they would do.

Fast-forward to 2016.

The banking scandal of the century unfolded as Wells Fargo was called on the carpet "for creating about $1.5 million in unauthorized deposits and 623,000 credit card accounts in customers' names without their knowledge." They also disclosed that they'd "previously fired 5,300 employees for their involvement in creating these fake accounts."[4]

But wait, didn't they say they would help their customers and be dedicated and constantly advocating?

They had forgotten all about their Business Ethos.

Wells Fargo had one last critical moment of opportunity. When the dumpster was catching on fire, they could have raised the white flag. They could have come clean—taken the mea culpa and leaned into their Business Ethos. They didn't.

Instead, the CEO covered it up, and the bank continued the illicit behavior. It took another year for them to admit to auto insurance fraud in 570,000 customer accounts, resulting in customers defaulting on car loans. Also, they "wrongly fined 110,000 mortgage clients for missing a deadline, even though the delays were the bank's fault."[5]

The Wells Fargo code of conduct reads, "Wells Fargo's reputation as one of the world's great companies for integrity and principled performance depends on our doing the right thing, in the right way, and complying with the laws, rules, and regulations that govern our business. We earn trust by behaving ethically and holding all team members and directors accountable for the decisions we make and the actions we take."[6]

Based on their behavior as a business, do you believe them?

I can't. Not only did they violate their own Core Values, but they covered it up instead of coming clean.

Every company makes mistakes. It's how you choose to handle them that matters. In this case, a more than 150-year-old business went up in smoke in a dumpster fire, all because of a failure to live up to its Business Ethos.

Mistake #3: The Feature Trap

Fact: it's easier to talk about your product than to talk about value.

Welcome to the **Feature Trap**. The slippery slope that is a race to the bottom.

When you're in the Feature Trap, you're "leading with product." Instead of thinking about the end result your customer wants, you skip to what you know—every single thing about your product. You're selling nuts and bolts, not security and safety. You're way down in the muck of what you do and how you do it.

It's hard work to tease out the bigger value or connection to the customer. Whether you're selling software or skincare, the easier path is rattling off a laundry list of awesome features about your product. "Lead workflow automation," "AI technology," "heated leather seats," "lowest cost," "organic ingredients"—they've got Feature Trap written all over them. When the leading lady of your script is your product, you're making it impossible for the right customers to choose you. There they are—trying to sift out why you're better, what makes you different, and why you are the best choice to solve their problems. Your customers can't see your business's value because they're blinded by product features.

The worst part is that the Feature Trap forces your customers to decide based on price. When a prospect can't see the value, you push them to choose based on price. When you push them to price, you push them to shop around. Now your ideal prospect is off considering your competitors, and your only choice is to cut your price and your margins. And the race to the bottom continues.

I got sucked into the Feature Trap recently.

I was assessing time-tracking tools for Growth Street. Knowing where our team is spending time gives us important profitability data and is key to optimizing our processes. I started by getting some referrals by reaching out to my network. To be honest, not one person said, "I love my time-tracking tool, and it's so worth the money!" Let's face it: time-tracking tools are a commodity—they all basically do the same thing—so if you're leading with features, you're pushing potential buyers, like me, into the muck.

So, off I went to do my research.

I looked at four different time-tracking tools: let's call them *Red*, *Blue*, *Green*, and *Yellow*. I looked for value and how they were different other than price. I searched for the Business Ethos. I turned over all the rocks. All I could find were features and prices across the board. No one was explaining the bigger business value. I finally picked *Blue* just to get it over with. I'm a busy person with a long list of things to do, and I don't have time to try to tick and tie your unique value together. Is *Blue* the best time-tracking tool to solve my problems?

I don't know.

I spend $100 a month, and *I don't know if Blue is the best choice.*

I'm pretty sure there was a better option, but I got so overwhelmed with features that I picked the one with decent reviews and called it a day. It wasn't because *Blue* spoke to my problems or told me why they were different; it was because I run a business and needed to decide quickly. Would I recommend *Blue* to you? I would tell you this story and send you on your way into the Feature Trap to decide for yourself. Is that the type of word of mouth you want to create for your business?

When you're in the Feature Trap, you're just one new feature or widget away from the competition eating your lunch.

Take Gillette, a once–*Good to Great* company. For decades, they led with product—from thin blades to double blades to triple blades, Gillette's entire strategy was product-led. They were in a footrace with Schick and Bic for decades, which eventually turned into a price war. Just when they thought things couldn't get more competitive, Dollar Shave Club launched on the scene and upended the entire industry.

Why did Unilever pay $1 billion at a 5X multiple for Dollar Shave Club, a start-up with a product that paled in comparison to Gillette and Schick? It wasn't about revenue or a superior product. It was because Dollar Shave Club had built a customer-obsessed brand. They knew their customers beyond "face value" (couldn't resist!), which meant they knew exactly what to say and do to attract customers and sell their products. Their storytelling speaks to a specific target market, and they are known for their cheeky videos that have gone viral, adding to the perceived value.

Dollar Shave Club knew that the only way to win in a product-led price war in a century-old industry was to avoid the Feature Trap and instead Differentiate by obsessing over their ideal customer.

The rest is shaving history.

Don't force your target market to figure out for themselves if you're the best choice for them. When you lead with product, price, and technology, you make your prospective customers do the hard work. And when you make your prospects work too hard, they might just look elsewhere.

Mistake #4: The Spaghetti Effect

Have you ever seen a two-year-old eat spaghetti? If so, then you've witnessed the **Spaghetti Effect** firsthand. I remember my kids learning how to feed themselves. My son was a wild eater. He would stuff his face, throw things on the floor, and occasionally throw spaghetti on the wall.

The funny thing about throwing spaghetti on the wall is that it doesn't stick. Maybe a strand or two, but most of it just slithers down the wall and falls to the floor.

The Spaghetti Effect is the business equivalent of my two-year-old throwing food at the wall. It's messy and haphazard, and in the case of businesses, it's also costly and ineffective. The Spaghetti Effect often happens when a business starts scrambling for a quick fix.

"Crank out more campaigns! More emails, more advertising, more, more, more!" I worked for a CEO who was king of the Spaghetti Effect. Revenue would be down, new account numbers down—whatever was down, he would come storming into my office. I was the CMO at the time, and he would shout (literally), "We need to pump out more emails! Why aren't we buying more ads? We need to try this new tactic *now*!" His ideas were not grounded in what would connect with our ideal customers, and the tactics weren't connected to the company's overall growth strategy. None of the spaghetti stuck.

Succumbing to the Spaghetti Effect is like jumping into a race car, flooring it, and hoping for the best. It's usually a crash and burn, not just from failed go-to-market attempts but from the stress and pressure it creates for the organization to try to make the spaghetti stick.

Here are some sure signs that you are throwing spaghetti. If you're:

- Chasing the competition and copying everything they're doing.

- Pumping out random marketing tactics—spraying and praying.

- Succumbing to discounts and offers every time you see sales drop.

As you'd expect, 99.9 percent of this race-to-the-bottom stuff doesn't work. Sometimes businesses get lucky. But luck is not a strategy.

Unrivaled companies do not rely on luck; they rely on a well-developed framework (which I will show you how to build in just a moment). Meanwhile, the spaghetti throwers are wasting time and money on stuff that's not going to deliver ROI. Even if it temporarily boosts sales, the bottom line will suffer, and long-term, sustainable business growth will grow further out of reach. It can also quickly lead to the Leaky Bucket.

Mistake #5: The Leaky Bucket

How much does it cost to acquire a customer? For many of my clients, their Customer Acquisition Cost (CAC) has at least two zeros, sometimes three. Let's just say it costs you $500 to acquire a bright and shiny new customer. And let's just say the Customer Lifetime Value (CLV) of each new customer is $100,000, meaning that over their lifetime they will generate $100,000 of revenue. So far, so good. You are laser-focused on acquiring new customers. You fill up your bucket with ten new customers—you're ringing the bell and hitting your revenue goals. Then, *bam*. All of a sudden, CLV is shrinking, CAC is rising, and you're left holding the bucket. What happened?

The **Leaky Bucket** is a sneaky problem. It's like a crack in your foundation—you often can't see it until you have a flood in your basement. The Leaky Bucket (also known as customer churn) happens when you spend time, resources, or money to acquire a customer and then they cancel their subscription, start buying from a competitor, and seep out of your bucket.

Leaks are expensive, and if you're suffering from the Leaky Bucket, you have two choices:

1. Stop the leak.

2. Pour more into the top of the bucket.

Remember our CEO who thought he needed a new logo to leapfrog the competition? Well, the actual diagnosis after talking to his past and present customers was that his business had a customer churn problem. He had a Leaky Bucket. Customers would award his business with multimillion-dollar contracts, but they didn't renew. They went out to bid with a competitor.

You might have a Leaky Bucket if your customers have:

- Little to no understanding of what your company stands for (your Business Ethos).

- Low or lack of ongoing engagement with your business beyond the sale.

- Negative interactions with your team.

- Poor issue resolution.

- High points of friction during onboarding, implementation, renewal, and other key customer milestones.

- Lack of emotional connection to your brand. (We'll return to this issue of brand a bit later.)

It's almost always cheaper to keep a customer than to go out and acquire a new one. As *Harvard Business Review* puts it, "Acquiring a new customer is anywhere from five to twenty-five times more expensive than retaining an existing one." Bain & Company research done by Frederick Reichheld, the inventor of the Net Promoter Score, shows that "increasing customer retention rates by 5 percent increases profits by 25 to 95 percent."[7] So why wouldn't you do everything in your power to keep those precious customers thriving, engaged, and happy—*in* your bucket? Our Unrivaled Growth Framework is a powerhouse at turning customers into happy, loyal, high-lifetime-value, obsessed fans. Rather than being a Leaky Bucket, your bucket overflows with customers and profits.

The Leaky Bucket often slips under the radar. Once a new customer comes in the door and we get them onboarded, we move on to the next new customer, and it's easy to forget to nurture the ones we worked so hard to get into the bucket in the first place. And worse yet, when prospective customers hear about the symptoms of the Leaky Bucket, it can make them less likely to give the company a try. Then the Leaky Bucket becomes a flood.

A couple of years ago I was serving as the fractional CMO for a software business that had recently gone through an acquisition and was struggling with some growing pains. As I turned over all the rocks, I noticed that they did not have an engagement strategy for current customers—nothing, nada. They were suffering from a major Leaky Bucket, and the competition was fierce to acquire new customers. When I raised the lack of an ongoing customer engagement strategy with the CEO, he said he had deprioritized it in favor of more "revenue-producing activities." Can you hear the record scratch? What is more revenue-producing than an existing customer? When I peeled back the onion and carefully probed his logic, he opened his mind to the conversation. He got up and went to the whiteboard, and we started doing the math on the CAC versus CLV. Within just a few minutes of some simple equations, he realized a huge revenue gap was staring him in the face.

You'll always have some element of churn in your business—that's natural. But the Leaky Bucket is when you have a systemic retention problem. Your most valuable, most profitable customers leak out of the bucket. At that point, it's like flushing dollar bills down the toilet. If you don't stop the leak, you need incredibly deep pockets to keep filling the bucket. Here's what I think of when I hear "churn and burn": churn the customer, burn the cash. You decide.

Mistake #6: The Moatless Castle

When Warren Buffett picks companies to invest in, he has one critical factor that he says is most important. It has to do with the durability of the company's competitive advantage, or so-called "moat."[8] In Buffett's world, the moat ensures that a successful business can stand the test of time.

"We're trying to find a business with a wide and long-lasting moat around it, surrounding and protecting a terrific economic castle with an honest lord in charge of the castle."[9]

All castles are subject to attack. It may not feel that way, but it is that way. Every day, a new business hangs a shingle ready to disrupt your industry and steal away your customers. When you sit back on your laurels—when you don't build and fortify your moat—you are giving competitors an opportunity to strike. Take a look at another former *Good to Great* business, Circuit City.

In the 1980s, Circuit City was the only big game in town. If you needed a TV or stereo, you either went to your local mom-and-pop shop or visited Circuit City. I remember going into Circuit City with my dad when it opened in our town. It was the early '80s, and he wanted to buy a VCR. We were swarmed by a bunch of sales guys in fancy blazers. They talked my dad through all of the features of this new technology that cost as much as a family vacation. They showed us how to use it and sold us an expensive service plan.

At the time, Circuit City was known for its high-touch service and expert salespeople. They were intentional about this sales and service model—it was their moat. They had crafted their competitive differentiator to focus on a specific target market: customers who didn't understand technology and who needed someone to talk them through it. Circuit City rode the technology innovation wave with its core business through the '80s to early 2000s. "Sales increased from $1 billion to $12.6 billion, earnings increased from $22 million to $327 million, and the number of stores increased from 69 to 616. In 1995, Circuit City entered the Fortune 500 at number 280, climbing as high as 151 by 2003."[10]

But then the castle came under attack.

While Circuit City execs were distracted, a Minnesota-based specialty audio store called Sound of Music decided to pivot. They hit pay dirt with a discount sales strategy and decided to rebrand and open "superstores" across the US. And just like that, Best Buy was born.[11]

Best Buy founder Richard Schulze was the epitome of Unrivaled. He let his Business Ethos of fairness and integrity guide his growth strategy, and he listened to his customers to stay in tune with what they needed. By observing his customers, he realized that they wanted a different way to buy. They didn't want salespeople hovering over them—they wanted to pick their products on their own and feel smart about their choices. They wanted to ask for help if they needed it—and feel like they were empowered to get a good deal. Best Buy embraced the changing customer demands while Circuit City stayed stuck in its ways. As Schulze wrote in his book, *Becoming the Best: A Journey of Passion, Purpose, and Perseverance*, "We had to rewrite the rules somehow—break away from the pack of look-alike competitors. We saw that our customers wanted a very different experience than our competitors were offering . . . We knew that our competitors in the consumer electronics industry were not delivering that experience, and that gave us a huge opportunity."[12]

Circuit City never saw Best Buy as a threat. "We thought we were smarter than anybody," says Alan Wurtzel, former Circuit City CEO, "but the time you get in trouble is when you think you know the answers."[13]

Circuit City failed to protect their moat. They got distracted by other projects like the launch of CarMax and a new DVD technology. They didn't see customers' expectations changing and missed the opportunity to keep their market leader foothold and expand their moat as the market was evolving.

By 2008, Circuit City was good to great to gone. (As I write this, they are trying to make an expensive comeback.)

Six Mistakes

Echo Chamber	Missing Business Ethos	Feature Trap
Spaghetti Effect	Leaky Bucket	Moatless Castle

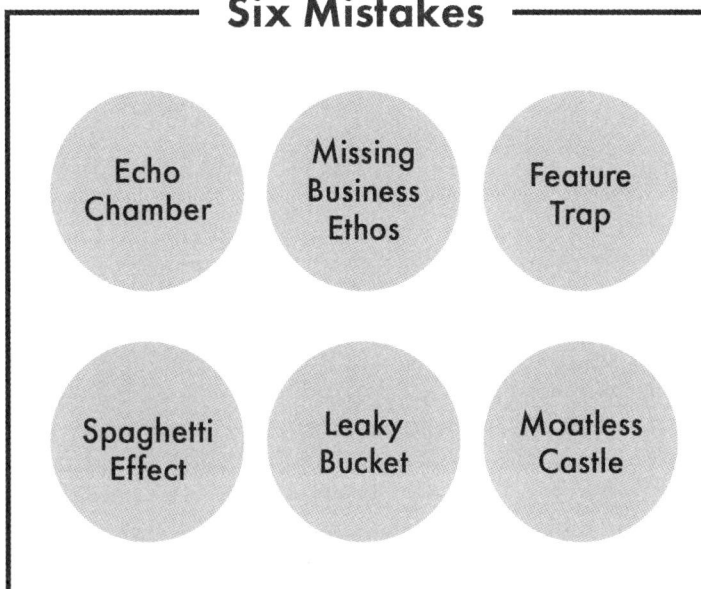

I want to help you avoid the "gotchas" that could be holding back growth. These six mistakes are probably responsible for 90 percent of what prevents businesses from achieving their growth goals. The good news is they are surprisingly easy to avoid. In my work with clients, both big and small, I have discovered that there are really just five simple steps necessary to avoid these dead ends, detours, and speed bumps—and to put yourself on the road to Unrivaled growth.

Ready to get started? *Giddy Up!*

CHAPTER 2
FROM HERE TO UNRIVALED

The GPS said: fastest route.

I was driving from Palo Alto to the San Francisco airport. Traffic was at a standstill. I was late.

I checked the GPS. It showed me a shortcut—this exit—right now.

I didn't have time to think. I turned off the exit.

The next thing I knew, I was at another standstill. Stuck in a detour. The GPS had no idea "the fastest route" was closed for construction. I was in a full sweat, further away from the airport, sure I was going to miss my flight. Taking immediate action might seem like a shortcut. But shortcuts turn into detours. And detours are expensive. They cost more resources, time, and money in the long run. Lots of businesses do first, think second. They are so deep in the day-to-day, they don't take the time to look up, ahead, and around the corner.

When you act first and think second, you lose control over reaching your destination. You might be lucky and make your flight. Or you might be stuck on the freeway as your flight sails overhead and your engine overheats.

But what if you had a framework that made every decision easier and every strategy aligned with your ideal customers? What if you were never in panic mode because your brand was so clearly and powerfully differentiated from your competitors that you left them in the dust? What if all your employees were so motivated to further your company's Mission that they became problem solvers and brand ambassadors? What if your go-to-market was effective and efficient? What if you could achieve explosive business growth by playing in a league of your own?

Welcome to the Unrivaled Growth Framework.

What It Means to Be Unrivaled

When you are the Unrivaled market leader, you are unstoppable. You've built a relationship with your customers that's turned them from buyers to raving fans. Those trusted relationships translate into sustainable business growth and Customer Lifetime Value (CLV). You've optimized Customer Acquisition Costs (CACs) because now you know who your ideal customer is, where to find them, and how best to connect with them. You're spending in the right places to get the right customer. Your team is more efficient because they're not all off doing a million different things, going in different directions. Everybody's focused on the same Mission. Everybody's saying the same message. Everyone's rowing in the same direction toward your North Star Vision.

When you achieve Unrivaled, you're untouchable. Your competitors can't beat you, because you're playing a different game. You're not talking about the same thing that all your competitors are talking about—while everybody else is talking about speed, you're talking about quality; while everybody's talking about black, you're talking about white. You're not playing defense, desperately fending off your competitors; you are playing offense, growing your business and igniting remarkable trust and loyalty with your customers.

The Unrivaled Growth Framework is a new way of thinking about how to create and maintain your competitive advantage to grow your business. When you do it right, it becomes a force multiplier. It's the secret to unlocking your business's full potential. It's the key to igniting explosive growth—whether that means going from $0 to $5 million, $100 million to $200 million, or $25 billion to $50 billion. This framework has helped my clients achieve all of these aggressive growth goals and more.

The Unrivaled Growth Framework also eliminates guesswork, cuts out wasted time, and reduces friction. Instead of throwing spaghetti, your go-to-market campaigns consistently and reliably deliver ROI. Instead of competing on price, you sell on value—and can charge a premium price. You stop overspending on customer acquisition and retention and are able to do far more with less. You escape what I call the "Sea of Sameness" and own a differentiated, market leader position. Instead of customer churn, you elicit loyalty and high CLV. And while others are struggling to grow, your business becomes an efficient and robust growth engine.

The Unrivaled Advantage

Throwing Spaghetti ⟶ Return on Investment

Competing on Price ⟶ Premium Value

Overspending ⟶ Do More With Less

Sea of Sameness ⟶ Market Leader Position

Churning Customers ⟶ High CLV

Struggling to Grow → Efficient Growth Engine

Sounds great, right? But how do you get there? Like any journey, you build a road map, and then you follow it. The devil, of course, is in the details. But don't worry: I have taken many companies on this journey, leading them to unprecedented growth, extraordinary multiples, incredible acquisitions, and fanatically loyal customers. For a cybersecurity start-up, I helped them unlock their Ownable Whitespace and go from the Sea of Sameness to Unrivaled, resulting in a 50 percent increase in pipeline and generating five times revenue.

For a commercial construction company, I used this framework to boost customer loyalty and tell the market a more differentiated story, helping their incredible team achieve a $1 billion revenue goal faster than they thought was possible. And for a financial services company, I built their Unrivaled brand from scratch to connect their powerful Mission with their ideal customers, resulting in growing assets under management (AUM) by 20 percent year-over-year and resulting in an acquisition by a top-tier financial services company.

Unrivaled Growth Framework™
Five Steps to Achieving Explosive Business Growth

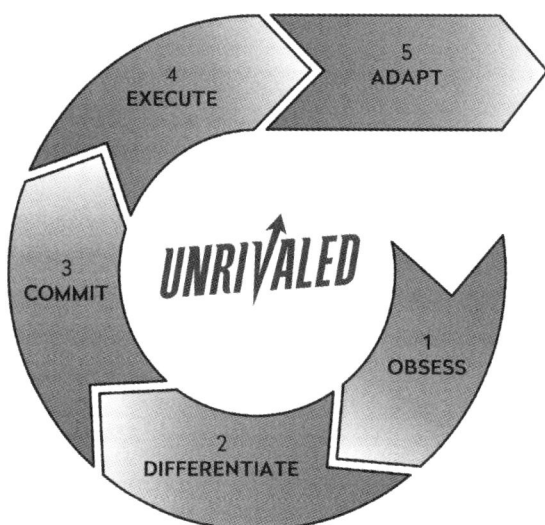

The Unrivaled Growth Framework: Your Road Map to Market Leadership and Explosive Growth

You know how some companies just make it look easy? As if double-digit growth and healthy margins are automatic? They seem to attract the best talent, beat their competitors to market, attract investors and VC money with ease, and create raving fans. That's what it looks like when you are Unrivaled.

When you go under the hood, you find some common denominators. A fanatical obsession with their customers. Clear differentiation about why they exist, what they stand for, and how they help solve customer problems in unique and appealing ways. Consistent messaging internally and externally, including a team that's fully committed to the company's Mission and Core Values. Go-to-market execution that delivers a "Surround Sound" experience for their customers. And constantly adapting to their ever-changing market and ideal customers to maintain their competitive advantage.

These are the core elements of our Unrivaled Growth Framework. In the chapters that follow, I'll explain how to implement each of these core elements using the five key steps.

Step 1: Obsess

For Unrivaled companies, everything starts with the customer. Not with your product, not with your innovations, not with your team, and definitely not with your logo. It starts by getting inside the mind of your ideal customer. You have to become obsessed.

If you build it, will they come? Sadly, this isn't a field of dreams. It's not good enough to build a better mousetrap and just hope the right buyers will discover you. Hope is not the answer. Getting inside the mind of your ideal customer is.

When I come in to help my clients, most of the time they have a decent understanding of their target market—the industries or demographics they are going after—along with some target market segmentation. But it's amazing to me how many companies cannot describe in detail who their ideal customer is.

Think of your ideal customer as the "bullseye"—like the center of a dartboard. A dartboard has lots of rings. And you get points when you hit the dartboard. You get *the most points* when you hit the center. Hit the bullseye. Ring the bell. Unlock explosive growth.

For lots of companies, they never ring the bell because they're trying to speak to too many different audiences—especially in the early growth stages. But to be Unrivaled, you have to point your arrow at the bullseye.

Who are your most valuable customers? Not all customers are equal. Typically, the 80/20 rule prevails—20 percent of your customers drive 80 percent of your revenue. In some companies, it's even more extreme—while I was a business leader at J.P. Morgan BrownCo, 90 percent of the revenue came from 10 percent of the accounts!

You need to unpack what your best customers care about the most. You have to adopt the words that appeal to them—and discover their hopes and dreams, their desires, their motivators, and their behaviors—so you can keep them, do more for them, and attract more of them. You might have reams of data about your customers. And while there's a quantitative aspect of knowing your customer, the data doesn't always tell you *why* someone bought something or what motivates them to buy a product or service like yours. So Step 1 in our Unrivaled Growth Framework is a deep dive into the hearts and minds of your ideal customer so you can hit the bullseye.

Together, we will clarify who your ideal customer is and unlock their mindset to tap into what they need, want, and care about most. When you Obsess over your customers, you are on your way to being Unrivaled!

Step 2: Differentiate

The business landscape can be brutal with the competition swarming, vying for the same customers, and clawing away your market share. Following Step 1 of the framework, you already have an advantage over many of your competitors: you know who your ideal customer is and what they need, want, and care about most. But to survive and thrive in today's climate, you must have an irresistible answer to a simple question: Why should they choose you?

It's a simple question, but the answer is almost always complicated. Buyers choose to do business with companies for a complex web of reasons. Not just because you offer a superior product or service, not just because you provide excellent value and outstanding customer service (note: you must, indeed, do all of those things)—they choose you because they believe in you, trust you, and want to do business with you. You're not selling; they are choosing.

So how do you stand alone and make it easy for your ideal customers to choose you? Step 2 in our Unrivaled Growth Framework is all about differentiating yourself from the competition. Done right, you not only become the number one choice for your ideal customers, but you create a new category that only you can own.

It starts with your Business Ethos. Remember, this is the soul of your business, the driving force behind why you exist. What's your Vision for a better world, and what's your role in making that Vision a reality? What are your Core Values—the principles you believe in that guide your actions?

I'm not talking about your business goals (not yet). Yes, revenue goals and KPIs are important. But your Business Ethos will clearly Differentiate you from your competition by telling the world what you **stand for**.

A powerful Business Ethos can help attract the right customers to your business, building rapport and trust. But to become your ideal customer's number one choice, you also have to solve their problem.

That's why a critical aspect of differentiation is to articulate why you are the best choice for your ideal customer and will solve a problem for them in a way that no one else can. I call this your Ownable Whitespace—the space in the market that only you can fill, the key that helps you **stand apart** from all your competitors. It takes you from being just one more player in a category to creating your own category—making your company the obvious choice for your ideal customers.

Step 2 of our Unrivaled Growth Framework doesn't stop there. I will also show you how to **stand out** to the world. This is where we talk about the image and public perception of your business that makes you the clear and compelling choice for your ideal customers. Remember our CEO who wanted a new logo? By Step 2, we know what that should look like. But this is not just about colors and fonts and a new logo design. In the chapter focusing on Step 2, you will get my specific, practical instructions for creating your Brand Manifesto, a complete playbook for all the customer-facing expressions of your brand to Differentiate your company.

Step 3: Commit

Your company's Business Ethos and Ownable Whitespace are not just important to your ideal customers. They also motivate and unite your internal team. Or not. To be honest, Step 3 is where most companies hit a wall—getting buy-in and consistent follow-through from the entire organization. It's not typically because of a lack of desire or good intentions on the part of your team—it's typically a lack of consistent communication down and across the organization about what your Business Ethos and Ownable Whitespace mean, both to your ideal customer and to each and every employee. We spend so much time thinking of ways to talk to our target market, we can easily overlook the people on the inside. If you don't have your entire organization fully bought into and aligned with your message and your Mission, and if they are not all rowing in the same direction, you'll miss out on reaching Unrivaled.

Our Unrivaled Growth Framework is a rallying cry for your entire organization, providing rocket fuel for your company's growth. That means every single member of your team has to be on board. Even one out-of-step employee can dramatically curtail your growth. To reach Unrivaled market leadership, every team member must talk the talk and walk the walk.

I went into a new client's office the other day, and I was talking to one of their project managers. I asked him what the company's Vision was. He said, "I don't know, but I think it's on a poster in the lunchroom."

Whoa. How can that company ever hope to become Unrivaled if their team members don't even know what they stand for?

Just imagine if every one of your employees were in lockstep with your Mission and your Vision. If each member of your team championed your brand and deeply knew your ideal customers—what they care about most, what they want, why they buy, what they need, how they talk—productivity would soar. Friction would disappear. In Step 3, I will show you how to get everyone to Commit and achieve alignment—that turns every member of your team, from the back room to the boardroom, into expert brand ambassadors.

Step 4: Execute

When I was in-house at Fortune 500 companies, we spent millions on "strategic planning." Supersmart people from big, expensive agencies and consulting firms came in to help us think. After months and months of long strategy sessions, they would deliver fancy pitch decks with creative concepts and ideas, but it was up to us to figure out what to *do*. We had all the ingredients for a beautiful seven-layer cake. But no instructions. When it came to baking the cake, we were on our own.

When I founded Growth Street, I committed to delivering strategy *and* execution—the recipe *and* the cake. So in Step 4, we Execute. I'll give you the ingredients and directions to successfully go to market. Together, we'll unleash the *Giddy Up!*—and let the horses out of the gate.

What do I mean when I say "Giddy Up"? I'm a big *Seinfeld* fan and always love when Kramer says, "Giiiiiddy Up!" It's that feeling of being super excited about something and ready to go do it. I guess I have a bit of Kramer in me! The *Giddy Up!* inspires my work at Growth Street and our unique blend of flexibility, excellence, and speed to achieve explosive business growth. And now I am sharing the *Giddy Up!* with you. The great news is that your hard work on Steps 1–3 of the framework sets you up for extraordinary success in Step 4. Together, we'll confidently put your Business Ethos and Ownable Whitespace into action by executing a successful go-to-market.

Your go-to-market includes all the ways your organization engages with your ideal customer to create trust and drive revenue. It's how you meet your ideal customers along their buying journey and deliver a Surround Sound customer experience that defines your brand in the marketplace. To reach Unrivaled—whether your go-to-market activities involve sales calls, product demos, social media posts, radio ads, emails, events, billboards, or any other tactic—they must all work together. Like individual musical instruments playing the same symphony.

A successful go-to-market creates beautiful Surround Sound music. It not only reinforces and magnifies every individual element; it also eliminates a whole lot of wasted time, effort, and money on marketing and messaging that don't fit with your brand. Every time your target market encounters your message or interacts with your brand, the core promise is the same.

Whether you're talking to an existing customer or prospective buyer, the look and feel are the same. The voice and story are the same. The details of the interaction might be varied, but your overall identity never wavers.

When you Execute a Surround Sound go-to-market, you have the key to unlocking high CLV and achieving Unrivaled business growth.

Step 5: Adapt

Like a shark in water, if you're not moving, you're dead. Even after you achieve Unrivaled status, you have to work to stay there. Times change, customers evolve, technology advances, new competitors jump in, supply chains get disrupted, costs go up, and profits start to shrink.

When Unrivaled companies face headwinds, they Adapt and adjust. Keep up. Stay relevant. Be efficient. I'm constantly helping my clients maintain their market leader advantage. Adjusting positioning. Making sure we still have Ownable Whitespace.

 Listening to customers' evolving needs and wants. Sharpening the messaging and optimizing go-to-market activities to meet the ideal customers where they are, in the words and ways that matter most. So the final step in our Unrivaled Growth Framework shows you how to *stay* Unrivaled. I'll explain how to Adapt and stay relevant as the business climate changes, new competitors emerge, and customers' habits evolve. Even when new threats and complexities arise, your Unrivaled Growth Framework will help you weather the storm. It's how market leaders Adapt and turn headwinds into tailwinds.

In my experience of talking to hundreds of CEOs from start-ups to Fortune 500s, I've found that many business leaders employ one or two of the strategies contained in my Unrivaled Growth Framework. But very few do them consistently, only a handful do them consistently well, and almost none of them put all five steps together into a coherent approach to everything they do. Until they work with me, that is! Once I show them the power of the framework and its ability to fuel explosive growth while reducing friction, waste, failure, and uncertainty, they are eager to get started on the road to Unrivaled. Which is what we'll do together right now. *Giddy Up!*

Unrivaled Growth Framework™

Five Steps to Achieving Explosive Business Growth

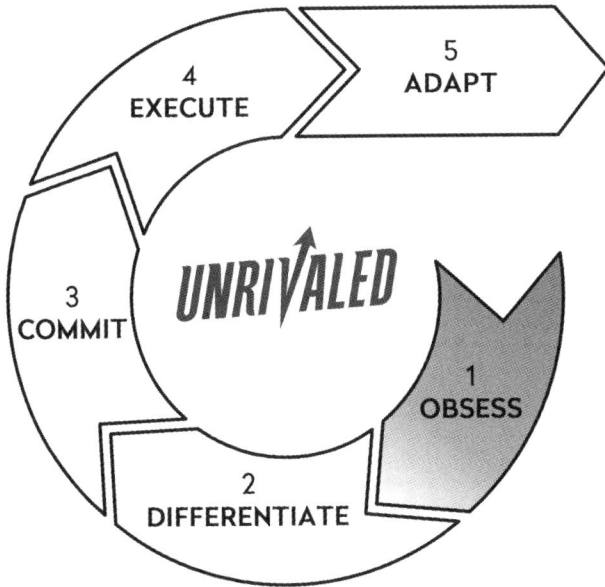

1 **OBSESS**
Clarify your ideal customer and unlock their mindset to tap into what they care about most.

STEP 1

OBSESS

"Get closer than ever to your customers. So close that you tell them what they need well before they realize it themselves."

—STEVE JOBS, COFOUNDER OF APPLE

CHAPTER 3

GET INSIDE THE HEAD OF YOUR IDEAL CUSTOMER

In 2011, Japan endured a triple whammy—a magnitude-9.0 earthquake that created a devastating tsunami that, in turn, caused an unprecedented meltdown of their nuclear power plant. The disaster claimed over twenty thousand lives, destroyed entire villages and towns, and challenged the country and its people to rebuild.

As they were rebounding from

Kizuna
"bond"

despair, Japanese businesses began using the word *kizuna* as a way to describe "the enduring bonds between people—close relationships forged through mutual trust and support."[1] The word became a rallying cry aimed at helping businesses create sustainable connections to fuel business growth. Soon, "kizuna brands" began to emerge. These were businesses that made kizuna a way of life—they built a bond of trust and support with their customers—resulting in unprecedented lifetime value, company culture, and brand affinity.

Subaru is a kizuna company. To them, the bond they have with their

customers is at the heart of everything they do. They have fostered raving "Subie" fans—earning them the highest overall brand loyalty of any automaker, beating Toyota, Honda, and Lexus multiple years in a row.[2]

It wasn't always that way.

Founded in the 1950s as part of the parent company Fuji Heavy Industries, Subaru was unprofitable for over forty years. They spent millions on R&D, releasing model after model, with a few peaks of success but mostly struggling to stay afloat and compete with the ever-changing car market. In the 1990s, after yet another failed attempt at juicing sales through a new luxury model and desperate to find a way to grow, the Subaru team made a series of bold moves to change what they were doing.

Instead of just churning through more meaningless campaigns and pumping out more makes and models, they decided to take a step back and focus on their customers. First, they admitted they didn't know their customers. Then, they decided to get inside their customers' heads.

Customer Demographics Are Not Enough

King Charles	Ozzy Osbourne
Male	Male
Born in 1948	Born in 1948
Raised in the UK	Raised in the UK
Married Twice	Married Twice
Lives in a Castle	Lives in a Castle
Wealthy & Famous	Wealthy & Famous

[3]

Starting with current customers, Subaru committed to better understanding who they were. They quickly realized they only knew basic demographic information such as age, zip code, gender, and household income. What do these factors tell you about:

- How a person thinks?

- What problems the person is trying to solve?

- What motivates and influences them?

- How they make purchasing decisions?

- What they care about in life?

- What matters most when they are buying a car?

They tell you nothing.

Surface demographics paint only a very broad picture. It's tempting to segment your customers at the surface level, but beware. It creates a false sense of security—you *think* you know your customers, but you actually don't. Would you serve these two people the same ad? I bet they don't occupy the same bullseye!

Their "stats" look exactly the same, but their attitudes, preferences, behaviors, and motivations are most likely totally different. Lumping prospects and customers into audience segments based on high-level demographic data not only tells you nothing about their mindset but can also steer your go-to-market efforts in the wrong direction and waste money.

Unlocking the ideal customer's mindset requires going deep into the gray matter—the psychographics of your ideal customer. This is where things like motivations, desires, goals, attitudes, preferences, interests, and behaviors live. Think of demographics as a black-and-white picture and psychographics as a full-color, 3D image. Here's what that might look like for Subaru's ideal customer:

Demographics

Married

$
HHI: $550k/yr

Attorney

45
years old

Lives in Virginia

Thrifty shopper who seeks value for her dollar

Listens to mystery, mom, and life coach podcasts

Eco-conscious and attends climate change rallies

Listens to Coffee House Rock on Spotify

Loves taking trips with her family and experiencing new places through travel

Likes brands that make her feel proud and safe—loyal to brands that earn her trust

Does lots of online research before making decisions and has very specific "must haves" when buying a car

A safe car is important as her daughter starts to learn how to drive

Volunteers at local dog shelter

President of her local women's chorus group

Psychographics

As you can see, diving into the psychographics reveals so much more than age, income, and other one-dimensional stats. Subaru's ideal customer starts to take shape as a living, breathing person—a confident and competent parent of a teen, involved in her community, dedicated to helping and protecting those who are vulnerable or less fortunate, who loves dogs and the environment and is attracted to both safety and quality. Now we see Subaru's ideal customer in 3D.

Understanding the psychographics of your ideal customer provides vital insights into why someone would buy your product or service, along with a treasure trove of additional information on where your ideal customers spend their time and how they make decisions. Unrivaled companies use this information to connect with both their existing and future customers at a much deeper level. This customer-obsessed superpower requires a commitment to regularly talking to your customers one-on-one—asking questions, listening to answers, following threads, starting conversations, and discovering new insights.

In other words, you need to be *obsessed* with your customers.

Subaru knew their customers bought their cars because of certain features, like all-wheel drive, but didn't know anything about the ideal customer's mindset. Why did they buy? What did they care about most? What made them tick?

They thought their customers were just an outdoorsy bunch, but as they dug deeper, they realized there was a powerful niche of educated, adventurous professionals who were raving Subaru fans. What was really interesting about this segment of their customer base—what distinguished them from the customers of other car brands—was that Subaru customers were also *eco-conscious* and *thrifty*, typically buying less car than they could afford. And over 30 percent of customers paid cash.[4]

Surfacing the buyer behaviors and motivations of their loyal customers opened the floodgates for the Subaru team. They started to understand their most valuable customers at a much deeper level—what they cared about, what mattered most to them. They quickly discovered new ways to talk to their target market, connect with future buyers, and meet customers where they were.

Subaru was able to streamline the buying process for the customer because of what they knew about their ideal existing customer—their raving Subie fans. Those valuable customers didn't need the incentives most other car companies were offering because their buyers were savvy and ready to purchase. This shift reduced buyer friction and juiced company profit margins, fast.

Subaru realized their customers valued the experience of the outdoors. Unlike luxury car buyers, Subies are "customers who are not buying things, but experiences," said Chief Marketing Officer Tim Mahoney.[5] Focusing on these mindset motivators was a major shift that propelled Subaru's success. They started playing up the adventures that customers experience with their Subarus and the connection between the car owner and the car.

A Breakthrough Moment

Then there was a breakthrough moment. Subaru followed the thread and started asking customers why they bought their cars. Typically, those answers included the standard stuff like safety, quality, all-wheel drive, and other feature-related feedback. But one thing kept coming up and triggered a light bulb moment for Subaru.

"If you'd ask a Subaru owner what they'd think about the car, the vast majority of the time they'd always answer the same way. Their answer was they loved it," said Alan Bethke, Subaru of America marketing vice president. "It didn't really matter what they had or who they were. The one thing that really kind of made [Subaru owners] the same was that answer."[6]

Love was the big idea that bonded customers to Subaru. It became the cornerstone of the Subaru brand. It gave them the power to grow through the 2008 recession, when most other car companies nose-dived. It helped them stay connected to their customers in real, meaningful ways and attract new ones.

Subaru's step back to get into the customer mindset resulted in a catapult forward. Subaru continues to achieve double-digit growth in sales along with recognition as one of America's best brands for social impact. Today, their demand exceeds supply, resulting in a decade of record-breaking sales increases.[7]

Subaru continues to earn high scores and top honors for customer loyalty by J.D. Power and was awarded the highest customer loyalty, 61.1 percent, in their category. Subaru of America President and Chief Operating Officer Jeff Walters said, "With the vast amount of vehicle choices available to consumers today, it is even more meaningful for Subaru to have such loyal customers as part of our Subaru family. We believe in our goal to be 'More Than a Car Company,' and the loyalty displayed by our valued customers reinforces the importance of not only providing a reliable product but also building a personal relationship."[8]

Had Subaru just looked at demographic data or some surveys, they never would have found the insights that unlocked the customer mindset and fueled a more emotional connection based on love. The Subaru "Love Promise" touches the customer's heart and creates a powerful feeling of kizuna.

Unlocking Your Ideal Customer's Mindset

You're probably wondering—how did Subaru get into their ideal customer's mindset, and how can I do that for my business?

Glad you asked.

My process for unlocking the ideal customer's mindset has been honed for decades. It requires putting in the time and effort to ask the right questions, dig into the answers, and follow the threads that surface insights to help your company bring your ideal customer to life. Once you do, you can connect with them in more meaningful and relevant ways.

So join me now as we get inside your ideal customer's mindset.

CHAPTER 4

FIRST, DEFINE YOUR BULLSEYE

Many companies I work with know *who* their most valuable customers are based on how much they spend, how often they buy, and other financial metrics. The question is: How well do you *know* them? To keep your best customers and to find more customers just like them, you need to get inside their mindset.

If you've ever played darts, you know how tough it is to hit the bullseye: that small red center of the board. I lost many a beer throwing darts at our local bar in college hoping to hit the red center and take double the points. Think about your ideal customer as the center of the dartboard—your bullseye. These are the types of customers you want to attract to your company. These are the people who need or want your product or service the most and who are ready to buy and stay with you long-term. These are the people who have the most revenue potential—your most valuable customers. This is where you want to point your arrow to achieve explosive business growth.

Sissy K's Knows Their Bullseye

Unfortunately, many businesses have been shooting arrows all over the place, sometimes for years. Arrows are flying over the cliff and into the dirt. Plenty of arrows just pop out of the bow and fall to the ground without even getting airborne.

Compare that to the genius of an iconic bar in Boston called Sissy K's. I love living in Boston. The city is life to me. There is so much history here and so much to do. I walk a lot and love to see local businesses in action. As I was walking through historic Faneuil Hall one day on the way to take my son to the dentist (you know, the glamorous CEO life!), I walked by Sissy K's. In their front windows, they display three simple messages:

- Kitchen open late.

- Karaoke tonight.

- DJ upstairs every night.

Pretty simple, right? Even if it's the first time you've ever walked by, you know exactly what they offer. Do you like, need, and want late-night food, karaoke, and a DJ? If your answer is "*Heck yes*," then you know this place is for you. If not, keep on walking.

The ideal customers for Sissy K's are people who love what they have to offer. I happen to be one of those people! That's why it totally spoke to me—I am in the juicy red center of Sissy K's bullseye. Karaoke, anyone?

Start thinking of your business like Sissy K's. Point your arrow at the bullseye. You don't need to appeal to everyone. You don't want to spend your marketing budget on everyone. Even companies with multimillions to spend are not targeting *everyone*.

The killer of joy is indecision. If you really want to grow, you have to be decisive. Focus on the bullseye and Obsess. It's time to go deep, not wide. You can expand as you learn—but don't bite off too much at the beginning. Focus on the bullseye so you truly become an expert at understanding them. As you have momentum going, you can start expanding out to the next ring of the dartboard.

Ask yourself these important questions to define your ideal customer bullseye:

- If we had to choose to focus on one segment of customers, who would it be? Why?

- Who are the people who need our product or service the most?

- Who are our most valuable customers today (profitable, loyal, influencers, and so on)?

- Is the customer we have today the customer we want tomorrow?

Defining Your Bullseye

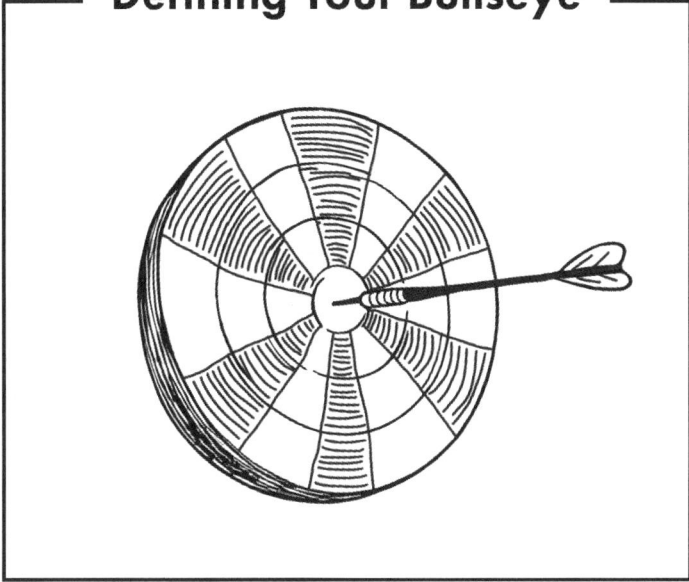

Armed with the answers to these questions, you'll start to see trends emerge—two to three customer types typically begin to bubble to the surface. When I do this work with my clients, the toughest part is choosing! Remember, when you try to serve everyone, you serve no one. Whether you're a new start-up or a one-hundred-year-old company, deciding who you best serve and who you want more of is growth power. Choose which ideal customer fits your bullseye. It doesn't mean you can't serve others; it just means that they are not your primary go-to-market focus. When you want to run an efficient go-to-market, it's all about using as few arrows as possible to hit the bullseye.

Now, take a moment to define your ideal customer bullseye:

1. If I had to choose to focus on one segment of customers, it would be: _____ because _____

_____

_____

2. The people who need our product or service the most are (describe the type of customer): _____

_____

_____

3. The most valuable customers today (profitable, loyal, influencers, and so on) have these traits (buying patterns, industries, sales cycles, purchase price, deal size): _____

_____

_____

4. Is the customer we have today the customer we want tomorrow? Yes___ No____ If no, how is the customer of tomorrow different?

_____

_____

5. Who are the customers we have lost but should have retained?

_____

_____

6. My bullseye is this type of customer: _____

_____

_____

This description forms the basis of your ideal customer persona, which will bring your bullseye to life. Let's dig in!

CHAPTER 5

CREATE YOUR IDEAL CUSTOMER PERSONA

Alan Cooper is widely known as the father of Visual Basic.[1] To me, he's the father of the persona. His book *The Inmates Are Running the Asylum* is on my bookshelf to this day, and it completely changed the way I think about customer focus as part of our Unrivaled Growth Framework. Cooper created personas as a way to empathize with and internalize the mindset of people who would eventually use the software he was designing.

A persona is an archetype of an ideal customer. While personas started as a design tool for software engineers, their power to enable customer obsession is unparalleled.

I learned the power of personas firsthand when I worked at Fidelity Investments, the financial services juggernaut and market leader. Fidelity was the industry pioneer of usability and user experience. They were known for their impressive Usability Lab—customers would come from around the world for tours—and innovation remains at the core of the company to this day. It has helped them gain the Unrivaled Advantage to play in a league of their own.

While I was at Fidelity, I was in charge of building digital products and experiences for their institutional customers. I would go over to the Usability Lab and spend time talking to the leaders there, learning how to surface customer insights into usable information. They taught me about human factors, user-centered design, design thinking, and more. One of the insights from this incredibly talented team was about the power of personas.

Before Fidelity brought people in for a usability test, they built personas that brought the customer to life. Prototypes and other assets were built to test and gather feedback. They talked to real customers and poured those learnings into everything they built. Over the years since I left Fidelity, I have evolved this persona creation into a revolutionary approach to branding, marketing, customer experience, and growth. It's part of my secret sauce that helped build the Unrivaled Growth Framework.

Building a persona is really just another way to bring your ideal customer to life.

- What are their goals?

- What are their problems and frustrations?

- What motivates them to buy?

- What other brands do they love?

- What do they care about the most?

- What is important to them as they make decisions?

- Where do they get their information?

- How do they make buying decisions?

- Whom do they trust?

Answering these questions and gathering this information takes time, but ultimately you will have an in-depth profile of your ideal customer, one that incorporates the psychographic elements you've uncovered and describes what really motivates and excites them.

At the outset, you might only have bits and pieces of the information in the sample persona shown below. And remember, this is not just a PDF; it's a shareable asset that helps your entire organization understand your bullseye at a much deeper, emotional, meaningful level.

Some of these elements you will be certain of, and others are assumptions. You'll want to validate any assumptions by talking to actual customers. (You know what happens when you make assumptions, d'oh!) Check your assumptions during the customer interview process (we'll

Example of Ideal Customer Persona

CEO Chris

Data-driven	Ambitious
Time-constrained	Collaborative
Confident	Competitive

"I want my company to be #1."

Age
48

Role
CEO of $50M tech company

Lifestyle
Lives in Palo Alto, CA
Married with a child and a dog

Goals
- Be #1 in their market
- Achieve aggressive growth goals to double revenue in 12 months
- Grow pipeline and win new business
- Stem bleeding from churn problem

Frustrations
- Hoped recent acquisition would fuel faster growth but isn't seeing the numbers
- Too removed from customers and not sure what they think/want/need
- Losing deals to new competitors
- Feeling pressure from the board to achieve aggressive goals
- Not sure that everyone in the company is aligned and rowing in the same direction

Interests
Traveling with his family, reading business books, coaching his daughter's soccer team, hiking with his dog, attending industry events, buying the latest tech, enjoying a glass of great scotch, working on his golf game with friends

Brands They Love
Titleist, Wall Street Journal, Fidelity Investments, BMW, Rolex, The Macallan, Apple, Robb Report

Buyer Motivations
Find new opportunities to grow
Build a stand-out company
Get results fast
Make decisions confidently
Use brand as a strategic lever
Be the market leader
Do things differently
Gain industry & peer recognition

Preferred Channels
Trusted peer network
Industry events/conferences
Podcasts
Email
LinkedIn
Social media
Internet search
Industry blogs & online publications

Chris's Story
Chris is a serial CEO. He climbed up the finance ladder and, after a number of CFO roles, stepped into the CEO position. He is an impactful executive who knows how to lead a team to success. He's had a few successful exits and is ready for another, though this one is proving to be a bigger challenge. Market headwinds are making it tough to scale to the next level and he's feeling frustrated with results. He's under tremendous pressure from the board and it keeps him awake at night. Chris admits that he hasn't been as close to the customer as he probably needs to be. He spends most of his time putting out fires, closing deals and satisfying board questions. He knows he needs a different way to look at solving the problem and is ready for some new ideas and thinking. He is at his wit's end and needs help fast.

66

I know this company is a winner. We have the best technology in our industry, but we're more like the best kept secret. I want my company to be the brand of choice for prospects. Building a brand is new for me and feels a bit scary, but I'm open to learning and challenging my preconceived notions.

© Growth Street

cover this in the next chapter), and dive deep into the psychographics to surface the behaviors, attitudes, desires, and interests of your ideal customer.

Business leaders often miss out on the value of personas because the name sounds like it is just an artifact. Plus, personas require some hard work to understand the customer at a deeper level. Doing this work separates Unrivaled companies from their competition. Customer obsession begins here by creating your draft persona—filling in as much as you can based on what you already know.

Now you're ready to road test your persona with real live customers.

CHAPTER 6

TALKING TO YOUR IDEAL CUSTOMERS

Once you have your draft persona, it's time to check your assumptions by actually talking to real customers. While it might seem obvious to talk to your customers, I will tell you that for many companies it is not. You might talk to your customers at an event or trade show or occasionally listen to prospect or customer calls. But that is not the type of talk I am talking about.

In my work with clients, there is often resistance when it comes time for customer research. I hear things like "We already know our customers!" or "Can we use the survey we did last year?" and "Can't you just listen to the call recordings?" While you might know your customers and have lots of tools to listen, there is nothing that replaces a one-on-one interview where you can ask the right questions. In most cases, companies don't know their customers in this deeper, mindset-focused way.

At Growth Street, we conduct "Voice of the Customer" (VOC)—a series of interviews with existing customers and prospects who match your ideal customer bullseye. VOC helps to check your assumptions, validate or disprove hypotheses, and bring your persona to life with more details based on what your ideal customers say—in their own words. Starting with the persona you sketched out, draft a list of questions for your interviews. You might need to adjust the script if you're interviewing multiple customer types. Think about everything you would want to know if you had an hour with a customer or prospect.

Here are some things to think about as you draft your interview questions:

- Where are there gaps in my understanding of my ideal customers—what don't we know?

- What assumptions do I need to validate concerning who they are or what they want?

- What hypotheses do I have that need to be proven or disproven?

- How does the ideal customer describe our company's value in their own words?

- What was the problem they were trying to solve when they first came to us?

- What appeals to them about my competition?

- Why did they choose our company? Or why not?

- Why would they buy again? Or why not?

- What do they think our company does better than anyone else?

- What emotional data can I uncover to win their hearts and minds?

- What don't I know about who my ideal customers and prospects are as people—outside of their jobs?

- What motivates my ideal customer to make decisions?

- What companies or products have earned their trust and why?

- What do they expect from our company that we are not delivering on?

- Where is there friction in the customer experience?

- Why would they (or would they not) recommend us to a friend or colleague?

Asking the right questions is essential to building out the details of your persona and surfacing the insights that will be key to achieving Unrivaled growth. Knowing what you need to surface in the interviews will guide the questions you ask.

As you're writing the interview questions, decide who you want to talk to. At Growth Street, we always recommend a mix of existing, past, and prospective customers. You learn different things from different customers at different stages of the buying cycle.

We typically suggest you interview five to seven of your best customers—those who come closest to your ideal customer persona. After interviewing five to seven people, you'll start to hear the same things, so it's most efficient to keep your numbers small. However, there are times when we interview five to seven people and determine we need to interview more people to follow the threads and gain the insights we need to truly hone in on our ideal customer bullseye. Remember, this is qualitative, not quantitative. You're having a conversation. If you're just starting your business, you might not have customers yet. In this case, create your ideal customer persona and look for people who meet the criteria. You can always go back later, once you've built your customer base, to refine the persona and add new ones.

The customer interviews we conduct are typically one-on-one interviews, thirty to forty-five minutes long, and done either face-to-face or via phone or Zoom. To unearth true customer gold, you have to be sure that whoever is conducting these interviews is:

- Unbiased and objective.
- Actively listening.
- Adept at knowing when and where to probe deeper.
- Surfacing key words and themes.

I typically recommend two people conduct the sessions—someone asking the questions and following the threads and someone taking notes and keeping time. And always record the session! You want to be able to go back and listen to the actual words they used.

When we conduct these interviews for our clients, I'm actively listening for opportunities to probe and go deeper. It's not enough to just ask the questions; you need to know when to follow the thread because there's more to learn. It's like a mining expedition—you need to always be on the lookout for a clue to unearth something valuable. Those valuable nuggets directly impact growth and the bottom line of your business.

Ninety-nine percent of the time, the things I hear during the VOC interviews are new insights for my clients. Sometimes those insights are high-five moments, and other times the insights illuminate gaps that might come as a surprise. The VOC might surface a customer perception problem, a poor product or service experience, a missed opportunity to connect with the customer, or other problems that are standing in the way of growth. I've conducted thousands of customer interviews, and there's almost always constructive feedback that reveals gaps in the customer experience. On the flip side, there are "aha" moments where we can literally hear the customer's delight and surprise and discover the things that keep them excited about the company.

Listen carefully to the words the customer uses to describe your company's unique value—it's solid gold!

Customer insights delivered firsthand are incredibly powerful, so be sure you mine them for all they're worth. At Growth Street, we create a detailed report of the key findings and recommendations and meet with the executive team to review them together. We have an open discussion, talking candidly about what we learned—the good, the bad, and the ugly. We identify opportunities for new experiences and products, we surface the words and values we heard, and we decide on gaps we want to close.

VOC unlocks a new level of innovation inside the company—from the outside in.

After your interviews are complete, go back to refine and flesh out the persona you started earlier. Now that you know your ideal customers better, add in the details you learned from your VOC, and give your persona a name (VP of Procurement Paula, CEO Chris, Sous Chef Sue, Director of HR Harry—you get the gist). Pick a memorable name that everyone in the organization can use, but avoid using actual customer names or photos or anything too specific to a customer. Choose an image that represents this ideal customer archetype and brings the persona to life as a "real" representation of your ideal customers.

Spreading Customer Obsession Throughout Your Organization

Unrivaled companies get the most out of their personas by sharing them with the entire organization. Giving your team—at all levels—insight into the ideal customer is essential to becoming Unrivaled. It creates a sense of common understanding throughout your company, driving innovation and building connections. It's also a great way to make sure you keep your finger on the pulse of your ideal customer as they evolve and change over time. When everyone on your team is customer obsessed, they can spot changes in customer behavior and identify opportunities to evolve and Adapt.

In many of the organizations I come in to help, only one department has a direct connection to the customer—for example, sales, customer service, or customer success. To achieve Unrivaled status, it's not enough for one department to "own" the relationship with the customer. You must create a customer-obsessed culture by sharing "Procurement Paula" throughout the company so everyone can understand your ideal customer's insights, needs, wants, and motivations. With this cross-company customer understanding, each member of your team can see their work differently.

When we did this work with one of our clients, a member of the team said, "I'm just a back-office person—my job doesn't impact the customer." After we completed the persona work, this same team member had an "aha" moment. She saw her job differently and within minutes identified several ways to improve the processes in her role to ultimately deliver a better customer experience. Not everyone is on the front line with the customer. Personas are the great equalizer. We have clients who have printed out their personas on large poster boards and hung them up in their offices, made laminated desk cards, included them in investor presentations, and started company all-hands meetings with personas to remind everyone who they serve. Personas are the gift that keeps on giving.

CHAPTER 7

THE POWER OF MEETING YOUR CUSTOMERS FACE-TO-FACE

I often meet companies that think they know their customers, yet they still have a growth problem. What I usually discover is that they have not done the work to get "up close and personal" with their ideal customer. They "know" them from afar, but how well do they *really* know them? Executives often think we can get the insights we need from listening to recorded customer service calls or interviewing the sales team. While there are most definitely learnings to be gleaned from these indirect channels, there is nothing like going directly to the customer. Only the customer knows the customer.

The financial services industry follows what are called Know Your Customer (KYC) rules. While KYC is driven in large part by anti–money laundering due diligence, it is also about the company's obligation to their clients. The company needs to determine suitability, which requires understanding each customer well enough to know which products and money-management strategies are appropriate and which are not. If you have a low risk tolerance, a financial professional should *know* you well enough not to recommend an aggressive investment strategy. While your industry might not be regulated to the KYC standard, there's a lot to be gained from thinking about how you could apply a KYC approach for your business.

When I was an executive at J.P. Morgan's active trader business, BrownCo, I led the team responsible for building the next generation of our active trader platform. At the time, BrownCo was the leader in the active trader business because of its coveted, high-value customer accounts. The firm had over two hundred thousand accounts that were carrying daily balances at least four times that of an E*TRADE account. (During my tenure, I was also part of the J.P. Morgan deal team responsible for E*TRADE acquiring BrownCo in 2005 for $1.6 billion.)[1]

As my team and I set off to create the future active trader experiences, we faced a challenge: we didn't really understand our customers at a deeper, mindset level. We were starting to ideate new platform features, products, and experiences, but we kept asking questions we couldn't answer.

"Is this new trading experience helpful to our ideal customer?"

"What do they love and hate about the current platform?"

"How do they use our trading tools in their day-trading lives?"

"How will this new platform appeal to prospective active traders?"

Our competitors all had lots of bells and whistles, and we wondered: "Does our ideal customer need or want those types of features?" We started making assumptions about our active trader customers and what they wanted and needed. Sure, we could listen in on customer service calls or meet some of them at trade shows, but we didn't *know* them.

As I was mixing and mingling with some of our most valuable customers during an event, I started going deep under the surface and getting to know them as people. I started asking questions about why they love to trade with us, what we could do better, and why they chose us over the competition. Suddenly, the customer came into view in a 360-degree way. More specifically, I realized that, in order to build the best online customer experiences, we needed to know:

- Why they chose to trade with us.

- What their trade desk setup looked like.

- How they used our products and platform.

- How they tracked their trades.

- What tools they used (both online and offline).

- What was missing from what they had today.

- What would make them more successful traders.

These are answers you cannot get from a phone call or survey.

So, I got an idea. I had read the user experience and usability teachings of Jared Spool, Alan Cooper, and Steve Krug (thanks to my amazing team of talented product, marketing, user experience, and usability experts!), and I thought—let's go into the homes of these active traders and see it for ourselves. We'll see their environment firsthand, meet them personally, and surface the learnings that will create future experiences for our best customers so we can keep the ones we have and attract more of them. Together with my incredible team, we came up with a game plan. But first, I needed to get our CEO on board. He was cautious and asked lots of questions. I was lucky because he understood the value of why we needed to try this approach, and I managed to get the lawyers to agree (still not sure how that happened to this day!) to let us go into some of our clients' homes and conduct interviews with them at their home-based trading consoles. And just like that, the "Where They Trade" Voice of the Customer study was launched. What we learned surprised all of us.

Before that project, we had a very different view of who we thought our customers were. As we move up in an organization, we often move further away from the customer. As an executive, it can be easy to get comfortable inside the walls of your office. At BrownCo, we thought these high-value traders were wearing expensive cashmere sweaters and Gucci® loafers and living in mansions. These were customers carrying million-dollar margin balances and running multimillion-dollar trading accounts, after all! But when we got to the customer's home, our assumptions were shattered. There'd be a beat-up pickup truck parked outside, and the customer would answer the door in a ratty old bathrobe (true story!). As he would show us around, we would see his trading setup—he was using a folding card table for a desk, two or three monitors hooked up to a hard drive, and three-ring binders of all the price history, but no fancy bells and whistles.

Who we thought our active trader customers were could not have been further from who they actually turned out to be.

As we went house to house and spent time with each customer, we started to identify trends. Personas evolved, and our ideal customer bullseye became clear. We heard firsthand why they were loyal to BrownCo, especially with the competition fiercely vying for their margin balances. We listened to their problems and understood their pain. We learned what mattered to them the most—and the least. As we reviewed and relayed our findings from the research, we realized that many of the ideas we had previously brainstormed needed to be left on the cutting room floor. They were not what the customer needed or wanted.

The "Where They Trade" insights changed our perception of who these customers were, and it allowed us to go much deeper in connecting with them because now we understood more about their psychographics—how they thought, how they worked, and what was important to them. We were obsessed! We were able to map to this deeper understanding, and it shaped the next generation of our platform. This ethnographic research was the first of its kind in the early 2000s, and I had the opportunity to share those robust learnings as a keynote speaker for several conferences focused on helping companies connect to customers. When your customer invites you into their home in their bathrobe—now *that's* Knowing Your Customer!

It may not always be feasible to go where your customer uses your products and services, but if you don't ask, you'll never know! You can say something in your ask like, "I am wondering if we might be able to meet you where you use our product so we can get a sense of how it fits into your day-to-day. Is that possible?" Even just a few "Where They X" insights are invaluable.

KEY LEARNINGS
FOR STEP 1

OBSESS

Becoming obsessed with your ideal customer is the first step in our Unrivaled Growth Framework. To recap the essential points, Unrivaled customer obsession means:

1. Going beyond demographics to discover the psychographics that drive your ideal customer.

2. Focusing on the juicy red center of the bullseye and not trying to market to everyone.

3. Taking the time to build your ideal customer persona so you really know the ideal customer you want to attract and retain (including giving them a memorable name).

4. Talking to your customers one-on-one to understand what matters most to them, debunk false assumptions, and hear the VOC.

5. Sharing your ideal customer personas with your entire organization.

6. Understanding how and where your ideal customers use your products and services.

How Customer Obsessed Is Your Company?

O	O	O	O	O	O	O	O	O	O
1	2	3	4	5	6	7	8	9	10

We don't know who our ideal customers are or how to reach more of them.

We know who our ideal customers are in terms of demographics, but we don't know their psychographics or what they care about the most.

We know our ideal customer, fully understand their mindset, and have developed detailed personas that our entire organization channels on a day-to-day basis.

How would you rate your company on the customer-obsessed scale? Take a moment to reflect on the process we've just walked through and give yourself a quick customer obsession score.

If you scored below a 4, get to work now on getting to know your ideal customers and committing to a customer-obsessed approach. You may not know your ideal customers well enough to win their hearts and minds. If you scored a 5 through 8, you still may be leaving profits on the table by not knowing what your ideal customers care about and all of the juicy psychographics that create the emotional connection that will allow you to maximize your bond with your customers.

If you scored a 9 or 10, high five! Keep up the great work—you're obsessed with your ideal customer and well on your way to Unrivaled growth.

Quick Wins for Customer Obsession

While it can take time to dive deep into your ideal customer's mindset and surface the insights that help you build robust customer personas, there are some things you can do right now to move you closer to Unrivaled customer obsession:

- Start listening to customer service and account management calls (live or recorded) to hear the customer's voice and words.

- Start baking some key value-driven questions into your interactions with customers.

- Go to review sites and see what customers are saying about you.

- Interview five of your ideal customers and ask about their frustrations, pain points, and motivations.

Now that you are on your way to being customer obsessed, it's time to unlock your unique competitive advantage and achieve the strategic differentiation that makes you stand out from the pack!

Let's move on to Step 2 of our Unrivaled Growth Framework: Differentiate.

Unrivaled Growth Framework™

Five Steps to Achieving Explosive Business Growth

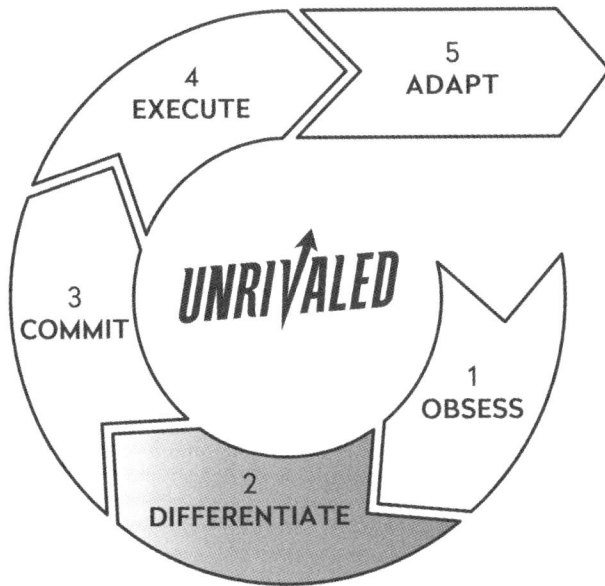

2 **DIFFERENTIATE**
Carve out Ownable Whitespace and sharpen brand differentiation to stand alone.

DIFFERENTIATE

"As of right now, you are nobody to everybody."

**—DAYMOND JOHN, CEO AND FOUNDER, FUBU,
AND COHOST OF *SHARK TANK***

CHAPTER 8

HOW WILL YOU STAND ALONE?

"Why would anyone pay $300 for a cooler?"

I was standing in front of a display of coolers at the general store in Quechee, Vermont.

My friend looked at me in surprise. These weren't just any ordinary coolers, she explained—they were the "Range Rover of coolers." YETI® coolers were known to be so indestructible that even bears couldn't open them, and they had a "grizzly-proof" certification. Customers bragged about their ability to keep ice cold for weeks at a time. YETI had raving fans consistently generating content—YouTube videos, blog posts, social media posts, and TikTok videos—and sharing their stories. What sounded almost like an urban legend to me was a trusted brand to their millions of obsessed customers.

YETI is an Unrivaled market leader.

How did YETI achieve their Unrivaled status? How did they transform coolers, travel mugs, and even pet food dishes into a status symbol? More importantly, how did they create such a high level of trust, brand loyalty, and value perception that their customers happily spend three times what a comparable item might cost? When your customers' buying behavior is no longer driven by price, you are in Unrivaled territory.

For YETI, it started by getting under the hood and learning everything under the sun about their ideal customer. Roy and Ryan Seiders, the cofounders of YETI, knew their customers' pain and frustration firsthand. As avid fishermen, they couldn't find a cooler that was heavy-duty and durable enough to not only keep ice cold for days but also support a three-hundred-pound person standing on top of it reeling in a line. They knew their market of hard-core fishermen, outdoorsmen, and wilderness lovers and channeled their ideal customer's love for hunting and fishing.

Then they took the next step on the road to Unrivaled: YETI carved out a space in the market where they stand alone, a unique and appealing way to Differentiate themselves from the competition. They resisted the lure of mass market retail and instead dedicated their attention to that avid sportsman and outdoor lover (their ideal customer bullseye). Focusing on that bullseye, YETI committed to a Vision, a Mission, and a set of values that matched perfectly what their ideal customers believed and valued. They focused on quality and durability even in extreme outdoor conditions (not fancy features, not price) as the hallmarks of their brand, delivering exactly what their ideal customers wanted most. And then they made sure that every single communication from YETI, be it a TV ad or the packaging on their labels, reinforced the brand they had built.

YETI has built a brand that stands for something their ideal customers (and employees) care about, that stands apart from all their competitors, and that stands out from the crowd. By doing so, they've created a thriving community of raving, loyal fans. The result? They *own* their category by redefining what buying a cooler means. YETI stands alone. YETI is Unrivaled.

Differentiate to Stand Alone

Step 2 in the Unrivaled Growth Framework is to Differentiate. Your goal is to make it easy for your ideal customer to choose you. To get there, you have to understand, articulate, and amplify what distinguishes you from every other choice your ideal customer has—*what makes you stand alone.*

In my work both in-house and with clients large and small, I've found that successful differentiation has three essential elements: you must **stand for** something your ideal customers and employees care about, you must **stand apart** from the competition, and you must **stand out** from the crowd in the eyes of your target market. Only by mastering all three elements can you truly achieve Unrivaled growth and stand alone.

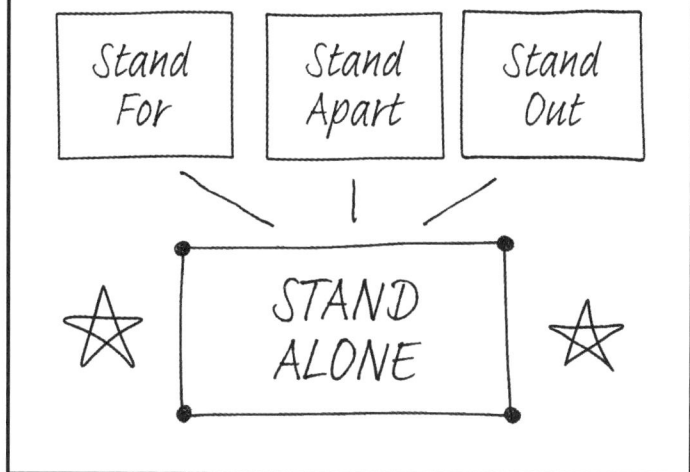

Unrivaled Differentiation
Elements for Success

Stand For — Stand Apart — Stand Out

STAND ALONE

Stand For: A differentiated brand starts with your Business Ethos. Remember the fatal mistake of the "Missing Business Ethos" from Chapter 1? When businesses fail to surface the Vision and Mission of the company and the Core Values that drive the company's actions and decisions, those businesses have a hard time connecting with their target market—and have little hope of standing alone. To successfully Differentiate yourself from the competition, you must explain why you exist—what fuels you to innovate and excel, what inspires you to serve your market, and what makes all the sacrifice and risk worth taking. Why you exist becomes a magnet for the right customers, employees, investors, and shareholders, providing the emotional connection people have with your business. Your Business Ethos is what you stand for.

Stand Apart: Once your Business Ethos is defined, you've got to separate yourself from the competition. You may have a bold Vision for the change you want to make in the world, but how does that specifically solve a problem your ideal customer (the bullseye) has—and why are you better than any of your competitors at solving that problem? Our

Unrivaled Growth Framework includes a new twist on traditional competitive analysis and SWOT exercises. The result: you are not just the leader in your category; you *own* your category. Unrivaled companies excel at identifying the Ownable Whitespace that makes them stand apart from the competition.

Stand Out: The final piece of strategic differentiation is presenting your unique value, your competitive advantage, your Vision, and your Mission to your target market in a way that drives home your unique identity. It's not enough to *be* different. You have to show and tell your target market, existing customers, past customers, and future customers that you *are* different. Based on those differences, your ideal customer will choose you—or not. I know this might be a controversial take, but a prospect not choosing you early is *good*. Don't spend the sales cycle if they know you're not the right fit for them. On the other hand, you don't want to miss out on the perfect customer because they don't know you exist, what you stand for, or why they should choose you. Creating demand requires standing out to the right buyer—your ideal customer. You become the chocolate to their peanut butter—you are, in fact, the perfect partner for them. To make this happen, you need a clear and comprehensive approach to convey your unique identity to your target market. Only when you clearly stand out from the crowd can you reach Unrivaled.

When you stand for something, stand apart from the competition, and stand out from the crowd, you stand alone.

You create Ownable Whitespace that no other company can occupy. You become the irresistible, unequivocal number one choice—the obvious and only choice—for your ideal customer. Instead of clawing for market share in a crowded competitive landscape, fighting for customers, and racing to the bottom on price, you play a different game and stand apart in a league of your own. You move from being just another company in a crowded field to being a *brand* that your ideal customer recognizes and trusts. We'll talk more about amplifying your brand in Step 4, but first, it's time to share my secret sauce for differentiating your brand to your ideal customer.

Giddy Up!

CHAPTER 9

KNOWING WHAT YOU STAND FOR: YOUR BUSINESS ETHOS

I went to an all-girls Catholic prep school.

I know, I know.

Stick with me here.

One of the things I will never forget is our freshman English class taught by Sister Evelyn. As a nun her entire life, Sister Evelyn was a great teacher. She knew how to keep us fickle freshmen on point—she even passed out candy during class. Sister Evelyn was a very thoughtful person and wanted us to get in touch with ourselves. I will tell you there was a lot of eye-rolling. Being introspective was not really a top priority for us fifteen-year-olds.

One of Sister Evelyn's tactics for getting us to think differently was to play music during class. She was known for playing the guitar or taking out her coveted record player. There was one song she played over and over—Diana Ross's number one hit: "Theme from Mahogany, Do You Know Where You're Going To." In the song, Diana Ross asks the listener insightful questions to reflect on their life and determine what they truly need. The point was to help us figure out where we were going in life. We would listen quietly and reflect on the words of the song and then share with the class. It felt painful at the time, but as an older, wiser version of myself, I not only appreciate Sister Evelyn's lesson personally, but I have put the principle to work every day, asking my clients these questions for their companies. If you don't know where you're going, how will you even know if you got there? If you don't know where you're going as a business, or if you don't have clarity and focus on the destination, your organization will never be aligned and committed to reaching your goals.

Building an Unrivaled Business Ethos

It's not as simple as writing down, "I want to become a billion-dollar company in the next ten years." If it were that easy, you'd already be there. Explosive growth and decisive market leadership require creating a brand that your ideal customers love and admire, that inspires trust and loyalty, and that overcomes competition and attracts the right attention.

Make no mistake: customers choose you, not the other way around. If your ideal customers don't understand who you are, why you exist, what you stand for, and why you're different, they don't know how to choose. When it's not clear why your company is the best choice for them, they are down in the muck and can only assess you on price. Selling on price is a race to the bottom. They will leave you as soon as budgets get tight or someone cheaper comes to town. If your go-to-market is all about the features and widgets, you'll be compared to that shiny new start-up that has all the features and widgets. Real customer loyalty is built on shared values. Buyers want to do business with a company that stands for something they care about (aka, your Business Ethos). Both customers and employees want to be part of something that has a larger purpose.

Your Business Ethos is not about checking a box just to say you have one. It's about using your greatest untapped asset—*what you stand for*—and bringing it to life. When you can articulate your Business Ethos, especially when you use words that resonate with your ideal customer, it's easy for people to join you because your beliefs align with their beliefs. You run a differentiated business that is grounded in purpose. "I've been a great believer in values through my entire CEO career because I believe values, Mission, and strategy are the most important boundaries you put into an organization," says former adidas® CEO Kasper Rørsted. "It defines a framework on how you operate and how you behave."[1]

Your Business Ethos has three components:

- ✓ **North Star Vision:** Your North Star Vision is the change you want to make in the world. It's a picture of a better world thanks to your company solving a big problem. Think of it as the ultimate destination. It feels far away, scary, and audacious—it's that bold.

- ✓ **Mission:** Your Mission is what your company will do to achieve that Vision. You know where you're going now, and you see a future in which you have solved a big problem for your ideal customers (and maybe for the world). What drives your company to get there? The Mission gets everyone in your company out of bed in the morning and working hard to achieve your North Star Vision.

- ✓ **Core Values:** The Core Values are the pillars that hold up your house. They are your belief system and part of your DNA: strong and unique, guiding what matters most to your company. How will you conduct yourself on the way to this better world? Your Core Values provide the guardrails to keep you from going off-track on your road to Unrivaled.

The combination of a North Star Vision, a Mission, and Core Values creates your Business Ethos and tells everyone who interacts with your business what you stand for. Together, they serve as a foundation for everything else you do. Just like the foundation of a house, they are sound enough to carry you through the storms and strong enough to hold the weight of whatever you build next.

Picture the Destination

To surface what you stand for as a company, start by answering this question: What change do I want to make in the world? It might sound grandiose, but the most successful companies—the Unrivaled companies—have a crystal clear Vision for how their company makes the world a better place. That destination becomes their North Star Vision.

I call it your "North Star" because it really does act like a compass for every future decision you make. Stay pointed toward true north, and you will reach your goal. Get offtrack, and you can find yourself stranded in the Sahara—or dangerously lost at sea.

An AI technology firm called AirWorks brought me in to help them. Their business was in delivering geospatial data intelligence to several industries including telecom, government, architecture, engineering, and construction. They had customers and a great product and wanted to accelerate growth. They saw the opportunity to not just be a player in their industry but to establish themselves as a market leader. They had aggressive goals, an incredible marketing leader, and an outstanding team. Together, we started the Business Ethos process.

As the CEO sat down, I told him this was going to feel a little bit weird. (Important sidenote: I had been working with this CEO, David Morczinek, and knew his style was very analytical, data-driven, and precise. North Star Vision requires putting aside data and quantitative answers, going way up, and getting what's in your head—out. To think about why you exist, the bigger problem you want to solve, and the different destinations you see and want to achieve. That jumble of words about the change you want to make in the world that free flows and kind of feels like nothing? I'm listening. Back to our story!)

Born at MIT and inspired by the advances in geospatial data collection and the power of AI, AirWorks had created a revolutionary technology for the built world. As I talked to David and his team about their Vision for the company, I could tell that it didn't come naturally to talk about what they stand for. This is the case for lots of companies, especially early-stage companies. There is so much pressure to build a product, show results, and prove it works, articulating a shared Vision is typically low on the list and takes a back seat to all of the other burning business priorities.

Is it more important to fix that product problem or articulate your Vision? The reality is that they are both important! Without a defined North Star Vision that everyone in your organization understands and believes in, how can you be sure you're headed in the right direction? You can't. Maybe you get lucky, but luck is not a strategy. Your North Star Vision is your compass that orients every member of your team and every decision you make.

In this case, David understood the value of articulating the company's Business Ethos, but his Vision for the company was living in his head. He knew where he wanted to go and what he wanted the company to stand for—he had tried to articulate it, but he hadn't been able to find the right words to share it with his organization and the world. I see this in many organizations. They are typically moving a million miles an hour with to-do lists and day-to-day responsibilities that make it almost impossible to think! Becoming Unrivaled requires thinking time and taking a pause in your day-to-day activities to go up to thirty thousand feet and see your business from a new perspective.

When founders, CEOs, and executive teams can articulate their North Star Vision, Mission, and Core Values, they create a shared purpose. It makes it easier to pull the right people in—employees, ideal customers, investors, shareholders, and partners. What you stand for is the heart and soul of your company.

I started by asking the toughest question, with thanks to Sister Evelyn and Diana Ross: Do you know where you're going to?

Your company can never get to Unrivaled unless you have a clear Vision of your destination and are able to articulate that Vision to the world. To achieve strategic differentiation, to truly stand alone versus all other competitors, you must stake out a destination for your company, a place high on the mountaintop that only you can claim. A place that looks very different from where you are today—a destination where you have changed people's lives, and—for them, at least—made the world a better place. In almost all cases, this big change you will make in the world happens through you solving a problem—a big problem—that your customers have.

Get Out of Your Comfort Zone

When I take my clients through this stage of our Unrivaled Growth Framework, it can sometimes feel a little woo-woo. I know I'm asking them to get way out of their comfort zone and focus on something completely different. But trust me, if you do this right, it will make every single decision your company faces easier and clearer.

I expect you have done some of this work, especially if you are the company founder. I often find that many businesses have tried to articulate their Business Ethos but maybe were only able to do bits and pieces. Maybe they started but couldn't find the right words and put it aside to come back to later. Every business leader has a dream of what their business can become someday in terms of both sales and impact. Now let's make that dream a reality.

CHAPTER 10

YOUR UNRIVALED NORTH STAR VISION

Close your eyes. I know this is going to feel uncomfortable, or even silly, but close your eyes. I want you to envision the destination for your company. The ultimate destination. I'm not talking about KPIs or numbers on a spreadsheet. I'm talking about the change you want to make in the world.

Pretend you got in a car, and you're driving on an open road. There's nothing around you. Where is your car taking you? Where are you going? And when you get there, I want you to imagine what this place looks like. Look around—what are the things that you see? Who are the people here? What does the environment look like? What do you feel? As you think about this North Star Vision for your company, you're looking that far ahead—at a destination that doesn't even exist in real life today.

When I went through this with David at AirWorks, he said, "I see a different world where we've paid attention to the climate and we've done things to help the environment."

"But what does that really mean?" I asked him. "What change are you picturing from the world we live in now?" So he said, "Well, right now, cities are congested, they're polluted, they're not great to live in. And based on population growth, we're not going to be able to grow housing in our cities fast enough to keep pace. So how do we build fast *and* responsibly?" Okay, now we're getting somewhere. I pressed him— take it up a level, go bigger. What is the impact that you want AirWorks to have on the world?

In a sense, your North Star Vision statement is your answer to *why you exist*. If your company doesn't exist to make the world better—or to make life better for your customers—you will always be pulling against the current. Trying to roll a giant boulder uphill.

Once you can articulate your Vision, growth gets easier. Actually, everything gets easier because you know where you're going—your North Star.

Solving a Big Problem

Sometimes, when a business leader gets stuck, I ask them to think about the macro problem. Why did you start this company? What were the problems you wanted to solve? Who do you want to solve them for? And how does all of that connect with the impact you want to make in the world?

So ask yourself this: If you could wave your wand and solve the biggest problem you can imagine, what is the problem? Solving that problem—a world without that problem—that's your destination. Your North Star Vision is bold. It has nothing to do with what you do or how you do it. It is why you exist—to solve the biggest possible problem and create an almost unattainable destination. It feels scary; it's that big. You might wonder if you'll ever get there, it's so big.

A few examples:

Nike: *To do everything possible to expand human potential.* Nike's Vision is not about athletic shoes or apparel. It's about a destination that makes a bold commitment (to do everything possible) to make a change in the world (expand human potential). The word choices really matter, and Nike does a great job of inspiring us with the word "potential" and creating an idea of bigger, greater with the word "expand." Human potential is the sum of its parts—not just every individual's potential but human potential as a cumulative force. The Vision is big—it feels almost unattainable. Are we ever done doing everything possible to expand human potential? Not in Nike's world.

LEGO®: *To inspire and develop the builders of tomorrow.* My kids played with LEGO sets for many years. LEGO taught them how to follow directions, accomplish a task, be creative, and so much more. We would sit at our kitchen table for hours building LEGO creations together. Named in 1934 from the Danish phrase *leg godt*, meaning "play well," LEGO's Vision is rooted in play. But they're not just making toys for kids. Their North Star Vision is pointed at the future, a future where today's kids playing with LEGO are tomorrow's builders of cities, airplanes, bridges, stadiums—and things we cannot even imagine. My kids, your kids, and the world's kids will literally build the future. All thanks to LEGO!

RTX Corporation (formerly Raytheon Technologies Corporation): *To make the world a safer place.* RTX is one of the largest aerospace and defense manufacturers in the world. Their North Star Vision centers not on jet engines, missiles, or satellites but on the effect they hope those products will have on the world. Making the world a safer place is like a beacon of hope and motivation—RTX will always be trying to achieve this Vision.

Darwin Trust Company: *To make trusts and smart money management attainable for everyone.* This was an inspiring North Star Vision to create together with my client, Darwin Trust Company. Where professional money management and financial trusts are not typically perceived as an option for most people because of minimum investment requirements, the Darwin Trust Company's North Star Vision points at "attainable for everyone," regardless of how much money you have to invest. The Vision also uses the word "smart," which was an important choice—it's not just *any* money management. It's *quality* money management.

Back to AirWorks. Their North Star Vision wasn't about AI and geospatial software. It was about a much bigger impact on the world—how we live as people in cities, towns, and communities and the contribution, as a company, that AirWorks can make to building better places to live. As I worked with David, the wheels were turning. He was communicating the words, I was asking the questions, and he trusted me and the process. He kept going—he told me it was about the cities, but not just cities; it's more. I kept guiding the process, and that's when he had the eureka moment. He saw the Vision clearly—the reason why they *had* to exist—and the words came out: "It's to build a more livable world."

Can you feel the goose bumps? This statement is AirWorks's North Star Vision—it is the change they want to make in the world. It is what they want to be. It is their guiding light and their true north.

It's not about selling software or building geospatial products. It's about a world where we build with people and the planet in mind. Where, as a company, we think about the impact our business has on people.

Bill Gates created one of the most successful software companies in history, but his North Star Vision for Microsoft was not about software. It was "a computer in every home and on every desk." Don't forget—it wasn't all that long ago that having a computer in your home was rare. Now it's as normal as having a refrigerator in your kitchen. Microsoft's Vision helped make that happen. What was so powerful about Microsoft's Vision was that Microsoft wasn't selling computers. They didn't make hardware. Yet Gates's clear Vision drove Microsoft to create a world where using a computer is a normal part of our daily lives.

Vision statements don't talk about what you do or what you sell. Your North Star Vision talks about something bigger—the reason that your business exists—the change you want to make in the world.

Bringing Your North Star Vision into Focus

To define your North Star Vision, start by asking these questions (or close your eyes and have someone ask them to you!):

- Why do we exist?

- What is the biggest problem we can solve?

- What is the change we want to make in the world?

- What does the ultimate destination look like? Feel like? Sound like?

Your North Star Vision should feel:

- Big.

- Bold.

- Audacious.

- Uncomfortable in a good way.

- Almost unreachable and scary—it's that big!

Sharing Your North Star Vision

Businesses are born from big ideas. Someone had a Vision and started a business. But as businesses evolve and founders move on, that Vision can get lost or forgotten.

Where does your business Vision live?

Let me guess: in your head. That's how it goes for most businesses. The business Vision lives in someone's head. The founder, the CEO—they have a Vision. A big idea to change the world. It's so big, it's scary. Which makes it hard to articulate. So it never sees the light of day. It just stays in someone's head. Most companies have a Vision, but the number one problem I see is that it hasn't been communicated out loud. Just because you have a Vision doesn't mean that everybody else knows it or understands it. And what happens when the founder leaves? How do you carry on driving toward the Vision? Your job is to make sure *everyone* knows the Vision and can see it just as clearly as you. They understand it and want to be part of it. They want to row in the same direction.

Without you defining and sharing your North Star Vision, your team can't see where you're trying to go. You're asking them to row the boat, but they can't see through the fog. One person is rowing in one direction and another in a different direction. You're missing the compass that points your organization toward a destination that truly makes a difference in the world—or at least makes your customers' world a better place.

Until you take it out of your head, you are the only person who can get you to the destination. If your team doesn't understand the North Star Vision—if they cannot tell it to somebody at a cocktail party—then you're the only person rowing the boat toward the Vision.

What does your North Star Vision sound like? Close your eyes and picture your ultimate destination past the horizon. Think of the North Star that guides your company and write what comes to mind.

My company's North Star Vision is:

_____

_____

_____

Once you have your Vision nailed down, share it with your employees, customers, investors, shareholders, partners—everyone! (We'll talk more about how to do this in Step 3: Commit.) Attract the right people who share your North Star Vision and want to be part of where you're going. Now, it's time to row ahead.

CHAPTER 11

CRAFTING YOUR MISSION

"I'm on a Mission!"

One of my clients said these words emphatically during a recent Unrivaled strategy session.

These words are visceral. You know what it feels like when you're on a Mission. You're unstoppable. Nothing can get in your way—you need to *do* it.

Your Mission Statement flows from your North Star Vision and is the driving force that guides what you do every day.

North Star Vision describes a destination that your company is committed to reaching.

Mission is what you *commit to do* to get there.

Think of your company's Mission as:

- The statement that inspires your entire organization to achieve your North Star Vision.

- Aspirational yet more grounded than your North Star Vision.

- Memorable and relatable.

- Passionate and emotional.

- The driving force that guides your decisions every day.

Something that ladders up to the North Star Vision.

How do you go from your North Star Vision to a Mission Statement that inspires you, your employees, your partners, your clients—and everyone you want to reach?

As I started guiding us to define the Mission for AirWorks, it was challenging to find the right words. I imagine my strategy workshops are a little like a songwriting session for Beyoncé. Getting the creative juices going requires opening the tap and letting the ideas flow. Getting the CEO talking and the executives contributing is when it gets really interesting. I'm listening and writing down words as they're talking. I'm looking for the threads and ways to turn words and ideas into lyrics—or, in our case, powerful statements and messages for the brand.

So the AirWorks North Star Vision is "to build a more livable world." Now the question is: *What will they do to achieve that Vision?* What will drive them every day to row ahead toward that destination? More specifically, what is special and unique about what AirWorks does that will help them get there? What will they do to create a more livable world?

Again, we started with some brainstorming. David said, "We want to power the built world." As we talked it through, we were still searching for a way to express their innovative contribution. "What's *unique* about your role in powering the built world?" I asked. "Well," he said, "providing data intelligence is a really important part of what we do." Okay, we were on to something. The marketing leader was at the whiteboard, the cofounder jumped in, and we started writing out the concepts and examining the components of their Mission.

You'll notice a key theme here about words. Pulling together the statements that make up your Business Ethos can feel like a word jumble—a free flow of words that are important to what you do every day. Then you put those words together to solve the puzzle and ladder back up to the North Star Vision. For AirWorks, every word or phrase had to be measured against this question: How does it lead to building a more livable world? Soon, the words were becoming a powerful statement that defined AirWorks's driving force. Together, we crafted their Mission Statement:

To provide the data intelligence that powers the built world.

Victory, high fives, jubilation. That's how it feels when we nail these statements. They're not just words on a page. They empower your business to greatness. They galvanize your team. They create purpose and connection. They open the floodgates to more revenue. They accelerate business growth.

One Mission Statement and Five Different Answers

Conduct an experiment—ask five different members of your team what the Mission of your company is. I'll bet you $1,000 you'll get five different answers. If Michael in accounting says A, John in HR says B, and Mary in operations says C, you've got a problem. Or worse yet, you face blank stares from Michael, John, and Mary. Everyone needs to know the Mission to live the Mission—the same Mission. Your Mission gets everyone rowing in the same direction toward your North Star Vision.

The good news is that your team can solve this problem together. Start talking about what you are on a Mission to do. What is the driving force that gets you out of bed in the morning? Just remember: every single answer to the question *What are we on a Mission to do?* has to relate back to your North Star Vision. So how does doing that help us achieve our Vision? How does it help us reach that mountaintop destination?

When I say that your Mission Statement is the statement that gets people out of bed in the morning, that makes them excited to come to work, that drives them, I mean it. In fact, a good Mission Statement is a rallying cry. It motivates and drives your entire organization forward. It gets everyone rowing in the same direction. If you're already doing it today, then that's not a big enough Mission. With any Mission, you're taking on something that hasn't been done—you're on a Mission! Your Mission Statement needs to be authentic and inspirational—it expresses what you want to do. It should be short and memorable so everyone in your organization can know it and live it. It should inspire every single person who works for you to reach that higher level. When they talk about their Mission, they feel like they're taking on a new challenge or they're doing things differently from how they have been done before.

From North Star Vision to Mission

Let's do some visioning and missioning together. This work can be challenging for companies to do. Sometimes Mission Statements sound more like Vision, or Vision sounds more like Mission—or worse yet, one doesn't connect to the other. When I get called in, I help companies sharpen these foundational elements. For each company below, I have taken their Vision and shown you how I would go from that Vision to a Mission Statement.

Nike: *Vision: To do everything possible to expand human potential.* **Mission: To bring inspiration and innovation to every athlete* in the world.** (*If you have a body, you are an athlete.) Nike's Mission is their driving force and ladders up to the North Star Vision of "expanding human potential." How will they achieve their Vision and reach their destination? By inspiring—and providing innovation to—every person in the world. Not many companies can get away with an asterisk in a Mission Statement. Here it is core to the Nike brand voice—almost like them saying, "Yes you!" Everyone is an athlete. Whether you're racing around the grocery store or running the Boston Marathon, you're an athlete in Nike's world.

LEGO: *Vision: To inspire and develop the builders of tomorrow.* **Mission: To be a global force for learning through play.** While other companies might seek to train builders, LEGO presents us with a unique and intriguing proposition: the way to develop tomorrow's builders is to teach through play. So, LEGO is telling their target market (and their team) that by becoming a champion—a global force—for the power of play to help us learn, they intend to inspire and develop children into "the builders of tomorrow." Notice the fun play on words—LEGO sees children as kids who will become builders in the future, and they also see them as builders of the future. Thanks to LEGO's approach to play, your children will build the world's future. Now that's got me buying more LEGO sets!

RTX Corporation: *Vision: To make the world a safer place.* **Mission: To build the most reliable defense and aerospace products and systems in the world.** For RTX, their Mission ladders up to their Vision, while at the same time it gets a bit more specific. They aspire to create the most reliable "defense and aerospace" products and systems in the world. There is a fine line in a Mission Statement where you want to get closer to the ground—more specific and tangible—but you don't want to get bogged down in the weeds of *how*. RTX walks this fine line, sharing enough detail to help us understand their Mission but still allowing us to dream of that safer world and see what they will do to get there.

Darwin Trust Company: *Vision: To make trusts and smart money management attainable for everyone.* **Mission: To empower individuals to secure**

their financial futures with compassion and care. As we discussed earlier, "trusts" and "money management" are not typically accessible to the average person. So how does Darwin Trust Company propose to change that? With empowerment, confidence, compassion, and care. First, Darwin tells us they will give individuals the authority and ability to handle their financial future. Next, they use a sacred word for finances: "secure." Already, I am feeling more confident about my future—Darwin Trust Company will empower me, and I will be able to secure my financial future! And then, to reach even higher, they promise to do so with compassion and care. The words "compassion and care" are incredibly important to the Darwin Trust Company brand. It's not just about money. It's about the driving force of empathy and meeting each person where they are on their financial journey. Most financial services companies do not use words like this in their Mission Statement, which creates a unique way to describe the company's driving force. It helps every member of the organization understand their Mission—empowering people, securing financial futures, and being caring and compassionate. The Mission helps to bring "attainable for everyone" to life in an inspiring and tangible way and ladders up to their North Star Vision.

What does your Mission Statement sound like? Think about the driving force that propels you toward your North Star Vision—you're on a Mission! Write what comes to mind. (This is a great exercise to do with your team!)

My company's Mission is:

_____

_____

_____

Without your North Star Vision, you have no destination. Without your Mission Statement, you have no driving force to get there.

With those two statements locked in, you can move on to the final component of your Business Ethos: Core Values—the intrinsic values that build connection, culture, identity, and trust.

CHAPTER 12

THE CORE VALUES THAT GUIDE YOU

When I was a young executive, I bought my first condo. It was in Boston's North End—the oldest neighborhood in the city—and it was during the infamous "Big Dig," a $25 billion project to move the interstate underground. The North End was tucked away under the I-93 overpass, and you had to take your chances "going under the bridge" to get home at night. My new neighborhood was under the shadow of the highway. It was the only deal left in the city.

The condo I bought was on a beautiful, tree-lined street, just a block from the waterfront. What I could see from the outside was a quaint brick building that looked strong and sturdy. The building was original brick and beam, and it was the most charming apartment I ever owned. Everything looked perfect.

What I couldn't see was what was happening underneath the building.

There was an issue with the foundation of the building. Buildings were starting to sink in our neighborhood—that's right, sink.

Back in the 1800s, Boston's North End was a mudflat—a stretch of wetlands. To create buildable land, the mudflats were filled in with sand and gravel to allow for expansion. Buildings were then constructed on top of wood piles called pilings. These pilings continue to support the buildings in Boston's North End today.

The gotcha is that pilings must remain submerged in water or the wood begins to rot. If you don't keep an eye on the water tables, your pilings rot and the building starts to sink. The same holds true for your business.

When most people hang a shingle and start a business, they typically just begin. They start building a product, selling a service, running promotions, and doing things with the hope of making the cash register ring. They don't stop and think about the foundation of the business—the heart and soul of what they believe and the Core Values they stand for.

Think of your Core Values as the pilings of a building. They are individual "pillars"—beliefs that work together. They are strong enough to support the weight of your business. They are essential to a strong foundation.

"You may think of Core Values as little more than window dressing or ticking a box without much real impact on the business," says Harvard Business School Professor Robert Simons. "But I've learned that the best companies—the ones that are most competitive and lead their industries decade after decade—put enormous emphasis on their Core Values and beliefs."[1]

Core Values are your business's belief system. They are a set of words that govern and guide your actions and decisions—think of them as guiding principles that cannot be compromised. They drive your company's culture, and every member of your organization lives and breathes them. They are at the core of your brand's identity.

Core Values are:

- **Foundational:** Strategic principles your company stands for.

- **Actionable:** Beliefs you not only say, but do—walk the talk.

- **Guiding:** Guardrails that guide decisions across the company.

- **Inspiring:** Motivating every member of your organization.

- **Connecting:** Meaningful to customers on an emotional level.

- **Differentiated:** Words that you authentically stand for that your competitors don't or can't claim. Together, they communicate the company's values to customers and help you stand out.

When customers interact with your business, they don't just care about your product or service. They care about what you believe in—they want to know if *you* believe what *they* believe. Does what matters most to *them* matter most to *you*? And every member of your organization wants to know what you stand for to see if you care about the same things they care about. Same goes for investors, partners, and shareholders. Core Values create a shared understanding of your company on a deeper, more meaningful level by showcasing the guiding principles you hold sacred.

Core Values are powerful and go beyond just an internal exercise. Your Core Values give your ideal customer a deeper view into the heart and soul of your business. They create the emotional connection and relevancy that provides you with an Unrivaled Advantage.

I encourage my clients to share their Core Values publicly. Unrivaled market leaders walk the talk. When you put it out there, you're accountable for delivering on what you promise. Find five to seven words (we want every employee to know these Core Values, and more than seven words becomes hard to remember!) that capture your Core Values and write a sentence to bring each of them to life.

Let me give you an example of Core Values in action using AirWorks. After we worked through their North Star Vision (to build a more livable world) and Mission (to provide the data intelligence that powers the built world), we workshopped their Core Values. The result was seven words that, together, define what the company truly values, which they also showcase on their website (as seen on the following page).

Culture & Values

AIRWORKS

At AirWorks, we are:

Customer-centric
We care about our customers and deliver value with every interaction.

Bold
We are undeniably curious and ready to enable the impossible.

Driven
We give our best because we want to be the best.

Accountable
We keep our promises, stand by our choices, and always learn from mistakes.

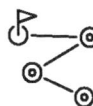

Nimble
We work quickly and strategically to problem-solve and reach our goals.

Collaborative
We work as a team, embrace our differences, and achieve success together.

Transparent
We keep it real by sharing information openly, candidly, and frequently.

What are your company's Core Values? Use a maximum of five to seven words that, when put together, create the guiding principles and inspiration for your business! Write what comes to mind (workshop this with your team).

My company's Core Values are:

1. _____

2. _____

3. _____

4. _____

5. _____

6. _____

7. _____

Your Core Values are the pillars of your Business Ethos. In my work with my clients, we have helped them embed their Core Values into the very fabric of their organizations, including:

- Adding them to the company's website.

- Baking them into performance reviews. (How does each employee embody the Core Values?)

- Building them into hiring practices to assess candidates on cultural fit.

- Creating Zoom backgrounds, screen savers, and desk cards. Including them in internal all-hands meetings and town halls.

- Launching a Core Values awards program and recognizing individuals for living a specific value.

- Creating a decision-making rubric using Core Values as guardrails.

Together with your North Star Vision and your Mission Statement, your Core Values form the rock-solid foundation on which your entire business can stand and grow.

CHAPTER 13

YOUR BUSINESS ETHOS IS YOUR ROCK-SOLID FOUNDATION

Building something that is meant to stand the test of time requires building a strong foundation. Luckily, my condo building caught the piling issue early. The damage was minimal, and we were able to quickly recover. You've always got to be checking your foundation for cracks or weaknesses. What you stand for will continue to evolve as your business grows, your customers mature, your market changes, and new competitors enter—change is constant. While your North Star Vision may remain unchanged, your Mission and Core Values need to Adapt as your business, customers, and market evolve. Revisit these core elements of your brand at least annually to make sure they are still relevant and differentiated.

The Key Ingredient: Emotion

As you're creating your Business Ethos, an important element of this work is getting emotional. In my work with CEOs and executive teams, emotion doesn't always come easy. Who wants to talk about how something makes us feel when there are numbers to hit and fires to put out? It can feel uncomfortable to focus on the feels. But think about how you feel when you interact with a brand that really resonates with you—you realize that they support the same causes you care about, they treat their employees with the same care and respect with which you believe people should be treated, and their Vision of a better world is important to you.

Business Ethos:
What You Stand For

	North Star Vision	Mission	Core Values
	30,000 ft	**20,000 ft**	**10,000 ft**
Defines	Why your company exists and the ultimate destination	What your company will do to reach that destination	How you will conduct yourself on the way to that destination
Creates	Beacon	Driving force	Belief system
Enables	• Alignment • Clarity • Purpose	• Empowerment • Focus • Efficiency	• Belonging • Empathy • Decisions
Looks Like	A short aspirational statement	A short empowering statement	5-7 words, each with a short description to bring it to life

When you crack through that tough outer shell of your business, you tap into the gooey center that is your company's heart and soul. In our daily left-brain lives of data, analytics, and logic, the Business Ethos work requires letting the right-brain creativity and emotion shine through. Your North Star Vision, Mission, and Core Values create a powerful emotional connection with everyone you want in your orbit—employees, prospects, customers, shareholders, partners, investors—they all want to share your purpose and bring your Vision to life. Consider Gallup's 70/30 rule—70 percent of decisions are based on emotional factors while only 30 percent are based on rational factors.[1]

Companies that connect with customers' emotions foster loyalty and have an opportunity to increase annual revenue by 5 percent.[2] What could 5 percent do to your bottom line? The rub is that only 15 percent of customers say that brands understand how to form an emotional connection[3]—that means 85 percent of companies have work to do! Are you ready to do the hard work and create a Business Ethos that emotionally connects with your ideal customer and inspires your entire organization?

Patagonia® is one of my favorite examples of a company that communicates its Business Ethos right to the bullseye of its target market. If you get the chance, look at their website—it includes Core Values, North Star Vision, Mission, and a clear focus on their ideal customer. Here are just some of the gems:

- "At Patagonia, we appreciate that all life on earth is under threat of extinction. We're using the resources we have—our business, our investments, our voice, and our imaginations—to do something about it."

- "Earth is now our only shareholder. We're standing capitalism on its head. The full value of Patagonia is now going to protect the source of all wealth—and our one and only home."

- "Our values reflect those of a business started by a band of climbers and surfers and the minimalist style they promoted in their lives and their sports."[4]

- "For our fiftieth year, we're looking forward, not back, to life on Earth. Together, let's prioritize purpose over profit and protect this wondrous planet, our only home."[5]

Hard but Worth It

Taking the time to articulate your North Star Vision, Mission, and Core Values requires a stop, drop, and roll. Who has time for that?

I get it. You're running a business. You've got investors and numbers to meet and a million things vying for your attention every day. And here I am, asking you to sit down and close your eyes—while your emails are blowing up, the board's asking for more data, and you've got employee issues to solve and customer fires to put out. I'm asking you to set all that to the side so you can think.

Seriously?

I'm dead serious. This step is not only valuable—it's imperative. You won't survive the economic headwinds ahead without it.

The bar has been raised. It's not enough to make great widgets and sell excellent products and services. Employees want a sense of belonging, to feel like they're part of a bigger purpose. Whether they are in the belly of the beast running the back-office operations or on the front lines with customers, they want to know they're serving something beyond just themselves. Customers also want to know what you really stand for. Are you just selling a widget, or are you trying to achieve something more impactful to society? Does that align with the way I see the world and my values? Do I want to work with you? Do I want to give you my money? Even investors are asking for it. My clients are constantly asked to provide their North Star Vision, Mission, and Core Values to investors and shareholders in boardrooms across America. In some cases, we've had to hustle, scrambling to figure it out to land new funding or close an enterprise deal. If you haven't been asked to share these fundamental elements of your business, I suggest figuring them out now so you're ahead of the game.

The truth is there's a whole ecosystem of people who are building trusted relationships with your business. Investors, employees, customers, partners, and shareholders. All these people want to know, when they get in the car with you, that you're heading to a place they want to go.

There are so many benefits you will reap from doing this work.

What you stand for is key to your strategic differentiation. It's part of what makes your company different from all others. Most organizations don't spend the time to articulate their North Star Vision, Mission, and Core Values. When you do, you are on your way to standing apart from your competitors. You have a unique advantage in hiring outstanding talent, retaining the best people, and attracting the right customers, partners, investors, and shareholders. And the list goes on. What you stand for is growth power.

Your Business Ethos becomes the ultimate decision-making tool. It helps you focus on the right customers, the right strategies, the right marketing language, the right hires, the right organizational structure, and the right growth plans. You will measure everything—and I mean *everything*—against the North Star Vision. Does this decision help us get there? Great, full steam ahead. Does this strategy align with our Mission? Perfect, let's do it. Does this partner share our Core Values? Boom, we're on board.

You will also gain tremendous efficiencies by what you say no to or *stop* doing. If a prospect doesn't align with your North Star Vision, hallelujah, you won't waste your sales team's time chasing the wrong customer. If a new product idea is not aligned with your Mission, you'll know enough to switch gears before wasting time and money. If a potential employee doesn't embody your Core Values, you'll avoid a bad fit and move on. Your culture will be purposeful and meaningful. Your team will be energized, aligned, and decisive. Your bottom line will be healthier from avoiding costly wasted motion.

Your Business Ethos delivers clarity. When you're clear about your North Star Vision, Mission, and Core Values, you have consistent messages that gain the trust of everyone you work with. Once you have established what you stand for in your ideal customer's mind, you don't have to keep selling them on choosing you every time. Your Business Ethos reinforces the purchase decision.

And one more thing. This work will give you a new measurement framework. You'll have a new way to measure employee performance and company performance. It takes the dollars and cents to another level and gives you new performance metrics that ensure you're actually getting where you're trying to go. For example, most of our clients use their Core Values as part of their performance review framework—either you're living the company's Core Values or you're not.

So, sure, you can skip this work. But you're likely to miss some pretty significant opportunities and make some painful, time-consuming, and costly decisions you could have avoided.

Our journey to Unrivaled is well underway. You've pinpointed your destination and made some commitments on how to get there. You've defined what you stand for and why you exist as a company. Now it's time for the second part of Differentiate: *standing apart* from the competition so you become the number one choice—the *only* choice—for your ideal customer. Ready to be the number one choice? **Giddy Up!**

CHAPTER 14

STAND APART: FINDING YOUR OWNABLE WHITESPACE

As a business leader at J.P. Morgan, I spent a lot of time traveling back and forth between Boston and New York City, participating in a variety of planning and strategy sessions. During one of these meetings, I sat next to a high-powered executive. She was impeccably dressed and carrying a coveted Hermès® Birkin bag. I was still climbing the ladder, and my paycheck was not yet enough for me to afford designer brands, but I recognized the Birkin bag immediately. The Hermès Birkin starts at $10,000 retail, with some styles going for upward of $150,000. Sotheby's recently sold a diamond-encrusted Himalaya Birkin at auction for $450,000![1] There are waiting lists to purchase one and long lines outside Hermès stores just to get a glimpse of the latest Birkin arrivals. When I complimented her on the bag, she said, "A Birkin bag is a great investment because it's Hermès, and that will always mean something special. Hermès always holds its value."

Do I think she was buying Birkin bags as an investment strategy? Heck, no. But her point has always stuck with me. The Hermès brand is unique. Every item is handmade, typically by one person at Les Ateliers Hermès, their workshop in Paris. Every item has a story and is designed to meet a specific customer desire. The Birkin bag has a story.

In the early 1980s, Hermès artistic director and CEO Jean-Louis Dumas was seated next to actress, singer, and fashion icon Jane Birkin on a flight from Paris to London. Birkin had just placed her straw traveling bag in the overhead compartment for her seat, but the contents fell to the floor, leaving her to scramble to pick them up. Birkin explained to Dumas that it had been difficult to find a functional yet stylish leather weekend bag she liked. She told him "the day Hermès [made] a large everyday bag that could hold all the items a busy mother carried, [she would] give up her signature oversized basket in its favor." Dumas sketched out the Birkin on the plane and took this encounter as inspiration to create the now-famous Birkin bag.

What gives Hermès the power to charge $10,000, $50,000, or even $150,000 for a handbag? They have differentiated themselves as the unquestioned choice for a very specific set of customers. They have not wavered from serving these discerning customers in a unique and special way since the company's founding in 1837. Countless competitors and new market entrants have come and gone in the last 185-plus years, yet Hermès remains relevant and revered. They continue to connect with customers—young and old—and stand apart from all competitors as Unrivaled.

For companies that are *built* as discount brands, such as a dollar store or T.J. Maxx, leaning into the low price and discount is what it's all about—it's *core* to their value and how they stand apart from their competitors. But that's not what differentiates a brand like Hermès. Do they ever have a sale? Never. Nothing is on sale. Ever. That is who they are. More importantly, that is who their customers trust them to be: so high-value that "discount" is a dirty word. If it's worthy of the Hermès name, it will always be full-price—that Birkin bag is $10,000, and it is always going to be at least $10,000, if not more![2] Buying the Hermès brand is a choice. You are telling the world: This brand represents me. I want the best, and I believe in this brand enough to pay $10,000 (or more) for a handbag.

When companies think about "differentiation," it's tempting to jump immediately to products, services, and price. If all your competitors are promising "the best" software solution, how can you gain market share without saying, "We have the best one too, but our solution costs less"? Competing on products, services, and price, however, is a race to the bottom—it's easy for a competitor to come along and undercut your price or launch similar product features, depriving you of your "competitive advantage."

In contrast, Unrivaled companies excel at distinguishing themselves from their competitors without resorting to discounts and special offers—instead, like Hermès, they use their unique value to stand apart in a league of their own.

Carving Out the Whitespace Only You Can Own

How can you get to the point where customers choose you based on something other than price—where price becomes almost irrelevant when compared to the value you offer your ideal customers? How does your target market see and hear you above all the competitive noise? How do you become the Unrivaled choice—standing apart so well and clearly from all competitors that you don't just lead a category—you *are* the category?

We've talked about how you can stand alone by standing for something—your North Star Vision, Mission, and Core Values. Now it's time to Differentiate yourself from all your competitors so you **stand apart**. As growth experts, we refer to this work as "competitive differentiation."

At Growth Street, we take a unique approach to competitive differentiation with a very specific end goal in mind: to create what we call your "Ownable Whitespace." This is the place in the market that *only you* occupy—a space that so perfectly meets your ideal customer's needs, no one else will do. You are not just your ideal customer's number one choice—you are their *only* choice.

Think of your Ownable Whitespace as the intersection of a) what you do best and b) what your ideal customer needs, wants, and cares about most, separate from c) what your competition does best. It is the culmination of all the work you have done in your competitive differentiation—a promise to your ideal customer that only you can make and that they deeply want.

Ownable Whitespace

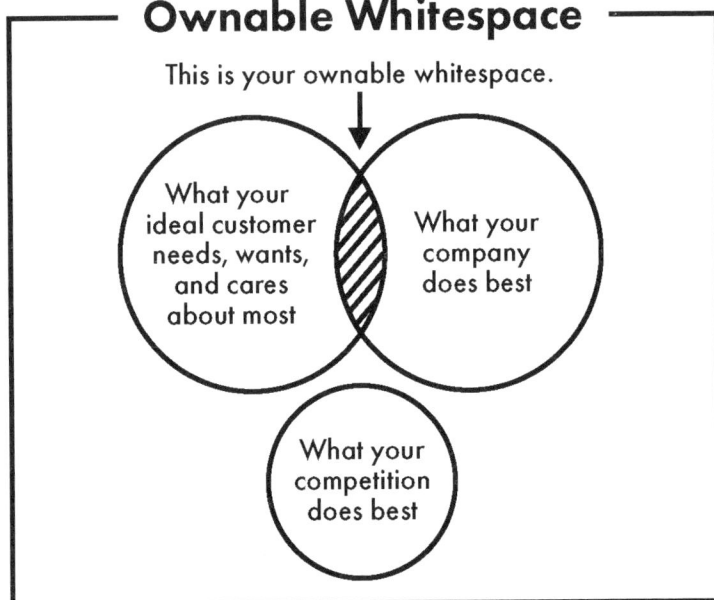

This is your ownable whitespace.

What your ideal customer needs, wants, and cares about most

What your company does best

What your competition does best

Finding your Ownable Whitespace starts with looking at your competitors through a new lens. Where is there room to uncover a new market opportunity, outmaneuver the competition, or stand apart in a crowded playing field? Then you "self-scout" what you do best and match that up with what your ideal customer wants (or needs) the most. You map that against the competition (both direct and potential threats) and identify the competitive differentiation that distinguishes you from everyone else. Your competitors can swim around you, but you create your own swim lane. Ownable Whitespace is the competitive differentiation that sets you apart and positions your company to be Unrivaled.

Let me show you the secret sauce we use to help our clients find their Ownable Whitespace and stand apart.

CHAPTER 15

LOOKING AT COMPETITORS THROUGH A NEW LENS

When I start working with a new client, I explain that you can't find your Ownable Whitespace until you truly understand the competition. After all, you can't stand apart if you're offering the same thing as your competitors. You have to study the terrain to find where you can occupy the high ground.

Most of the companies I work with have robust competitive matrices that catalog pricing, products, features, and funding and can be pivot-tabled, sliced, and diced. When I look at these documents, they are almost always missing some key competitive insights that are key to helping ensure they stand apart from their competitors.

You may think you know your competitors well, but do you know them beyond funding, products, features, and price? It's time to shift your thinking about your competitors and understand them at a deeper level. When you want to be Unrivaled, you must ask a different set of questions:

- What are your competitors claiming as their main benefit or value to their customers?

- Who are they trying to pull into their net—their ideal customer bullseye?

- What words and statements do they use to describe why they are different?

- How have they positioned themselves in the market?

- What is their North Star Vision statement—the better world they seek to create?

- What is their Mission Statement—their description of *how* they will create that better world?

- What Core Values do they stand for?

- How do their customers describe their value?

We typically document this scouting work in a spreadsheet by creating columns for the bullets listed above. Look for the words your competitors use to describe why they are different, their unique market position, and the benefits to the customer. Include as much information as you can—a lot of it is readily available on their website. Listen to their podcasts. Review their white papers. Check out their case studies. Watch their videos. Check their social media. Read their blog posts and press releases. Pay special attention to their customer testimonials and reviews—that's where you find what their ideal customers value most, in their own words.

You might be wondering what this special competitive lens has to do with identifying your Ownable Whitespace. Unrivaled companies make a strategic decision to be different. Instead of following the crowd, they carve out their own playing field. If you want the Unrivaled competitive advantage, you need to deeply understand your competitors to find space to stand apart. If you want to turn your customers into such loyal fans that they no longer even consider buying from someone else, then you have to really understand what attracts potential buyers to your competitors. This new competitive perspective gives you differentiation power—as Siimon Reynolds says in his book, "When they zig, you zag."[1] Unrivaled companies have a zag mentality—they carve out the Ownable Whitespace that sets them apart.

From Sea of Sameness to Standing Apart

I came in to help a $30 million SaaS software company. Revenue had plateaued, and they were throwing spaghetti at the wall hoping something would stick as they tried to find new ways to grow. When I dug into the

Ownable Whitespace process with them, there was an audible "aha" moment. As we were drilling down on each of their competitors—they had Fortune 500 goliaths and dozens of start-ups crowding the market— we discovered that they were talking about the same unique value as their competitors. They were stuck in the Sea of Sameness—a dreaded place where your ideal customer can't hear you because you sound too similar to your competitors.

Without a clear Ownable Whitespace that stands apart, it's easy to fall into the Sea of Sameness. Over time, your brand can start to look and sound like everybody else's—like all the other companies in your competitive set. When everybody is saying the same thing, your ideal customer doesn't know why to choose you versus the competitor down the street or across town. When you're in the Sea of Sameness, the only way for your customer to decide is based on price. The Sea of Sameness makes it hard for sales to do their job. It wastes marketing dollars, and it gives customers a reason to choose your competitor—they don't see, experience, or feel the difference. Instead of zigging like everyone else in the Sea of Sameness, find your zag—the Ownable Whitespace only you can claim—and stand apart to your ideal customer as the obvious choice.

What Your Competitors Do Best

To make sure you're out of the dreaded Sea of Sameness and standing apart, it's important to know what your competitors are saying and doing. The key to making this competitive analysis meaningful is to dig beneath the surface. You are on a treasure hunt looking for what drives customers to choose your competitors over you *and* to understand the Whitespace they own so you can steer clear. You want to uncover what your competitors are promising their target market and what their customers are saying. Focus on benefits, not features; focus on problems solved, not product stats; focus on the specific words your competitors are using. The prize in this treasure hunt is pure gold: discovering that clear Ownable Whitespace for you and you alone.

Oftentimes, a company's "about" page will shed some very interesting light on how they view their position in the marketplace. What do they say about their North Star Vision and Mission? What are the key benefits they promise? What type of customers are they trying to attract? This work is about reverse engineering to find opportunities to stand apart.

I also recommend that you widen your net on who a "competitor" is. Beyond your top three to five direct competitors, scout out your indirect competitors: companies that could be a threat down the road if they got an infusion of funding, for instance, or someone who occupies an adjacent space now but could easily introduce a new product or service that competes head-to-head with you in the future. Being Unrivaled means staying ahead of the competition today and creating Ownable Whitespace that becomes a protective "moat" tomorrow.

As you do this competitive analysis, you'll start to see your market differently. Instead of just seeing product, price, and features, you'll see how your competitors are positioned, which ideal customer they're trying to attract, and what they're doubling down on in terms of their unique value. What Core Values are they talking about? What benefits are they emphasizing? Speed versus quality. Service versus price. Wide selection versus carefully curated. Understanding how your competitors are differentiating themselves can open up a huge space in the marketplace for you to occupy and own.

Now it's time to understand your competition and the Whitespace they own. Dig into what your competitors are saying and doing.

My top direct competitors are:

_____

_____

_____

My indirect or potential threat competitors are:

_____

_____

Who my competitors are trying to attract (their ideal customer):

_____

What my competitors say they do the best:

_____

Things my competitors say to describe their differentiation, unique value, and market position:

_____

Words my competitors use that I need to avoid:

_____

In many cases, you'll find that you're using words your competitors are using—the Sea of Sameness—like my SaaS client above. But have no fear. That's why you're here! You now have a powerful new way to look at the competition so you can take action to stand apart in a league of your own.

CHAPTER 16

UNLOCKING WHAT YOU DO BEST FOR YOUR IDEAL CUSTOMER

Once you have discovered what your competitors do best and the Whitespace they are trying to own, you're ready to look in the mirror and define what you do best for your ideal customer. Our approach is laser-focused on zeroing in on the benefits that only you can provide to a very targeted, ideal customer. From there, you can successfully carve out *your* Ownable Whitespace.

Warby Parker is a great example of a company that has successfully carved out their Ownable Whitespace by doubling down on what they uniquely do best for their ideal customer.

My daughter needed reading glasses at a young age. Anyone with kids knows how fast they grow. I was spending thousands of dollars on glasses as her prescription was changing all the time, along with her personal style. If you wear glasses, you're familiar with the lousy experience of buying them: you go in to see an optometrist, they give you a prescription for glasses, they have a crappy selection of ugly frames in their office—and you spend four or five hundred dollars on a pair you don't even love.

Warby Parker comes along and says, "We're going to build a company that solves this problem and understands the customer's desire for a better experience, a better selection, and a better price." They know what their ideal customer needs, wants, and cares about the most. Busy moms like me want to be able to order a pair of glasses online so my daughter could try them on at home, and then send them back and place the order. Or we can go into the store and have a delightful, seamless experience. (The Prudential Center store in Boston is outstanding!) Warby Parker's service is flawless, regardless of channel, and they have nailed the customer experience.

As an ideal Warby Parker customer, their story speaks to me:

"Every idea starts with a problem. Ours was simple: glasses are too expensive. We were students when one of us lost his glasses on a backpacking trip. The cost of replacing them was so high that he spent the first semester of grad school without them, squinting and complaining. (We don't recommend this.) The rest of us had similar experiences, and we were amazed at how hard it was to find a pair of great frames that didn't leave our wallets bare. We started Warby Parker to create an alternative . . . We believe that buying glasses should be easy and fun. It should leave you happy and good-looking, with money in your pocket."[1]

Warby Parker took a commodity (eyeglasses) and turned it into a great customer experience. They don't talk about product features. They talk about what they do best and what matters most to their ideal customers. That's how you shift the purchase decision from price to value. And this is how you achieve Unrivaled.

Defining What You Do Best

Rather than trying to be everything to everyone, Unrivaled companies become the *only* choice for their ideal customer bullseye. The key is knowing what you do best and finding the space that only you can occupy.

When I do this work with clients, I usually gather the executive team in a room and hand out sticky pads and markers. My first instruction: "Write a sticky note for everything your company does the best. You have five minutes."

This exercise is to get the wheels turning and juices flowing. It's not about arriving at a perfect answer. Here's a prompt:

Off the top of your head, what are the three to five things your company does better or differently from your competitors in terms of delivering unique value or benefits to your ideal customers?

1. _____

2. _____

3. _____

4. _____

5. _____

I work with clients all the time to help them get these words out. Together we articulate, assemble, and create the strategic differentiation that makes their companies Unrivaled.

Once the five minutes are up, we put all the stickies on the wall and start to organize them by themes. We'll typically see lots of overlap—are there words that everyone listed? Are there common trends or threads to pursue? Are there opportunities to lean into certain strengths that our competitors don't have?

Pull out your competitive analysis and match up what *they* do best against what *you* do best. Where's the overlap? Where's the opportunity?

According to a 2021 study, "88 percent of marketers . . . aren't confident their buyers understand what makes their solution unique."[2] If your buyers can't quickly grasp why you are different from your competitors, you're likely wasting marketing dollars and sales motions.

And remember: trying to be all things to all people is a recipe for failure. Keep your eye on the bullseye—your ideal customer—the person whose problem you are uniquely qualified to solve.

What Does Your Ideal Customer Need, Want, and Care About Most?

Remember all the great work you did in Step 1 of our Unrivaled Growth Framework? It's time to put that to work here. By obsessing about your ideal customer, you have a clear idea of what motivates them, what their problems and needs are, what factors go into making them choose you.

Using your ideal customer persona, what are the three to five things they need, want, and care about most when they shop for and buy a product or service like yours?

1. _____

2. _____

3. _____

4. _____

5. _____

I was going through this exercise with one of my clients when we had an "aha" moment. Speed was something the company did extremely well *and* something their ideal customer wanted most—and it was Ownable Whitespace. Speed was something none of their competitors claimed or talked about. The company knew they were actually a lot faster than most of their competitors. Was it also the reason people chose them over anyone else? For someone in their target market who was in a rush or on a deadline, you bet.

In some cases, you might list benefits that several competitors also offer. Let's stick with speed. Let's say you are fast, but so are several of your biggest competitors. Now it's time to go deeper. What kind of speed do you offer? Maybe it's speed with accuracy, speed with confidence, speed with quality, speed with clarity, or speed with no wasted time or effort. Be as specific as possible about those benefits—until you get to a space that no one else occupies. It's the spot in the marketplace where you are the obvious first choice for your ideal customer. No one else will do, because no one else offers the perfect match between your unique benefits and the needs of your ideal customer. This is your Ownable Whitespace.

Your Unique Value Proposition Is the Articulation of Your Ownable Whitespace

You might have heard of the term Unique Value Proposition (UVP). In our Unrivaled Growth Framework, your UVP is the articulation of your Ownable Whitespace. It is a short, differentiated statement that articulates the Ownable Whitespace only you can claim. This powerful declaration is an expression of what your company uniquely does best and what matters most to your ideal customer, in their words. Your UVP keeps you out of the Sea of Sameness and is the differentiated statement that you'll use in your go-to-market across all channels, such as on your website home page.

Unique Value Proposition (UVP)

It is a short, differentiated statement that articulates the Ownable Whitespace only you can claim.

This powerful declaration is an expression of what your company uniquely does best and what matters most to your ideal customer.

Here are a few UVP examples from some well-known companies that have done a good job of carving out their Ownable Whitespace and articulating it to their ideal customer:

- **Gong:** Turn customer interactions into team productivity.
- **Trader Joe's:** The best prices on the best products every day.

- **Canva:** Easily design anything.

- **Mint:** Experience a fresh way to manage money.

- **Starbucks®:** Expect more than coffee.

- **HubSpot:** Grow better.

Now it's your turn. Define your company's UVP. Start by filling in the elements of your Ownable Whitespace:

What my company does best: _____

_____

What matters the most to our ideal customer: _____

_____

What we do or offer that our competitors *don't*: _____

_____

Next, distill this into a single, powerful sentence—a truly unique proposition that expresses your company's unique value and clearly describes, in your ideal customer's words, the Ownable Whitespace that only you can claim:

My company's UVP is _____

_____

Your UVP tells your ideal customer why you are the obvious choice!

Don't Get Smoked by Your Competitors

One minute, you're the only game in town. The next, the competition is swarming. One minute, you own your category. The next, you don't. One minute, you're budding with business. The next, the buds are sitting on the shelf.

When a product offering is new, it's often easier to stand out. Take the cannabis business. A few years ago, cannabis became legal here in Massachusetts. There was a huge supply and demand problem—too much consumer demand and not enough licenses to grow and sell.

With little to no competition, the early cannabis brands were flying high. They had Ownable Whitespace to spare. Their unique benefit was simple: Want weed? Come to us.

Fast-forward to the "ganja glut." New cultivation licenses in Massachusetts started being approved quickly, quadrupling the growing capacity. New retail brands were popping up on every corner. All the same products, just being sold by a different brand.

Suddenly, competition increases, prices drop, and customers have choices. How will they choose you?

Don't get smoked by your competitors. As new competitors jump into the pond, be sure your Ownable Whitespace is powerful and clearly differentiated from your competition. You have to regularly ask: What's the competition saying, and do we still have clear Whitespace in the eyes of our ideal customers?

Now that your Ownable Whitespace is clear and you've articulated your UVP, it's time to create the playbook to stand out. ***Giddy Up!***

CHAPTER 17

YOUR PLAYBOOK FOR STANDING OUT IN A CROWDED MARKET

As we have discussed, Unrivaled companies achieve powerful competitive differentiation by:

- Clarifying and committing to a North Star Vision, Mission Statement, and Core Values—a Business Ethos that explains what you **stand for**.

- Finding your Ownable Whitespace, where you are not just the leader of a category, you *are* the category—and capturing that in a powerful Unique Value Proposition (UVP) that helps you **stand apart** from the competition.

The final piece of Unrivaled differentiation involves building your playbook for communicating all this wonderful uniqueness to your target market so you can **stand out** to your ideal customer.

Too many companies rush to market without this playbook, which can cause a lot of wasted time, effort, energy, and dollars on marketing that doesn't work and messaging that doesn't stand out and speak to their ideal customer. It's like a hockey team taking the ice without a game plan. Your players don't know what to do. Your right wing doesn't know who to pass to, and your center isn't in position to redirect the shot into the net. Meanwhile, the other team keeps slapping the puck into the goal—making the siren blare and the red light flash.

Unrivaled leaders (like the best coaches) have a playbook. They draw up a winning game plan so every play makes sense—the whole team works together to score and win the game. Just like a championship team, Unrivaled companies use this playbook every time they take the field. Internal and external messaging is consistent and perfectly aimed at the ideal customer bullseye. And the entire go-to-market, including all your marketing and sales campaigns, continually illustrates and reinforces your Ownable Whitespace.

The benefits to this approach are incredible. Your go-to-market efforts are effective and efficient—no wasted budget! You deliver a consistent experience for your ideal customer that turns them into loyal, raving fans who will drive invaluable word-of-mouth growth. You stop throwing spaghetti at the wall searching for something that sticks—instead, your entire go-to-market cuts through the noise and connects with the ideal customers you want to attract and retain. Your entire company is aligned and rowing in the same direction. People know what to do and feel inspired to do great work—achieving company goals happens easier and faster.

Your Brand Manifesto

At Growth Street, we call this playbook your **Brand Manifesto**. In addition to your customer persona, your North Star Vision, your Mission Statement, your Core Values, your Ownable Whitespace, and your UVP, your Brand Manifesto will include the following "customer-facing" elements:

- Your positioning statement.

- Your story.

- Your voice.

- Your Visual Identity.

Brand Manifesto

```
                    Mission
                    Statement
        Story                      Voice

Unique Value                              Positioning
Proposition                The            Statement
                        Components
Visual                  of Your Brand      Core
Identity                                   Values

     North Star                      Ownable
      Vision                        Whitespace

                Ideal Customer
                    Persona
```

Writing Your Positioning Statement

The overall job of your Brand Manifesto is to steer how you *communicate* to your audience. And not just communicate, but communicate effectively. Consistently. Persuasively. Compellingly. Distinctively.

Remember, your North Star Vision, Mission, Core Values, and Ownable Whitespace are all components of your brand that have to be shared with your ideal customer in a way that is meaningful to them. That's what your positioning statement does. Think of it as your "elevator speech." A clear, concise statement of typically two to four sentences that explains, "why you?" and causes your ideal customer to say, "Hey, this is interesting" or "Wow, sounds like exactly what I'm looking for!"

When I work with my clients to craft a positioning statement for their brand, here is the formula I use:

For (your ideal customer): _____

_____

Who (describe need or want): _____

_____

(Company name) is (UVP): _____

_____

That unlike (describe competitors): _____

_____

Delivers (differentiation or reasons to believe that set you apart):

_____

There is typically a process of refinement that happens as we build your positioning statement together. Getting it right is one of those "aha" moments!

Remember the demographic and psychographic diagram we created for Subaru? Based on that, their positioning statement could look like this:

- For: Working moms of teenage kids
- Who: Want to love their car and know that it's safe
- Subaru is: More than a car company
- That unlike: Other car brands
- Delivers: A "love promise" to be a positive force in the world and empower those most in need while creating driving experiences that are safe, enjoyable, and memorable.[1]

Breaking it down further, it's all about word choices:

For (*ideal customer*) **working moms of teenage kids**: It's not just any women or any working moms. Being more specific about teens is an important distinction for Subaru. It helps them think about how to better reach these incredibly smart, accomplished, busy, adventurous people.

It also speaks to the unique challenge of parenting new drivers. (I have now been through it twice, and it's one of the most terrifying and exciting moments in your life as your child takes the wheel of your car.)

Who (*describe need or want*) **want to love their car and know that it's safe**: Love is central to how their customers feel about their cars. At the same time, they have new drivers on the road and want to know they are safe in the car they choose.

Subaru is (*describe Ownable Whitespace*) **more than a car company**: They know their ideal customer has lots of choices. Subaru uniquely positions their Ownable Whitespace beyond the car to win ideal customers for life. "More than a car company" tells their ideal customer that it's not just about providing a safe and reliable product but also about building a personal relationship. Their kizuna continues to shine through in their powerful UVP!

That unlike (*describe competitors*) **other car brands**: Of which there are many!

Delivers (*unique benefits or reasons to believe that set you apart*) **a "love promise" to be a positive force in the world and empower those most in need while creating driving experiences that are safe, adventurous, and memorable**: Subaru doesn't talk about features. Instead they talk about delivering a "love promise" and emotionally connect to important psychographics for their ideal customers, such as making the world a better place and helping others. At the same time, they use words like "safe" and "adventurous" to reinforce what they do best.

What's Your Story?

Everyone loves a good story. Research shows that people remember stories twenty times more than facts alone. Your company has a story—why it was founded, how it came to exist, and the journey that has brought you to where you are today. It's not a timeline nor a recap of events. It's a strategic narrative that conveys the essence of your company's DNA. So, let me tell you a story.

I was traveling for a client and got in a Lyft to head to the airport.

The driver asked me what I did for work. I told him I help businesses solve challenging growth problems. He told me he was starting a real estate business and asked if I would give him some advice. I said, "You've got twenty minutes."

He told me he'd been advised that you can't grow a business without a big marketing budget. That without the ability to spend hundreds, thousands, millions, he wouldn't be able to grow a thriving business.

News flash: a big marketing budget is not the answer to growth.

I asked him *why* he started the business.

He told me about his grandmother losing her house and how he felt so much shame. He felt responsible because he didn't know how to help her financially. He told me that he wanted to help other people avoid the same situation. By the end of the story, he was in tears, and so was I.

He said, "So what should I do?"

I said, "Tell that story."

He looked at me in the rearview mirror, surprised and a bit confused. I told him that he was already ahead of the game because he had a meaningful story. My new friend hugged me as he dropped me off at the airport. I thought about how lucky I am to impact someone's life by helping them think differently about growing their business.

Just like with my Lyft driver friend, the goal of your story is to build an emotional connection with your ideal customer. Your story helps them understand who you are, why you exist, and how you came to be. And by "you," I mean your company. By sharing your initial Vision, and then the journey you have taken to achieve that Vision, you help your ideal customer see what you saw when you began. No business story is perfect, so don't be afraid to share some of the twists and turns along the way! Being transparent and authentic builds trust and helps future customers understand you better.

Imagine you've been invited to do a live Q&A on stage at a major trade show. Your company has just won an award for excellence in your industry, and the moderator welcomes you to the stage, invites you to sit on the comfy couch opposite him, and asks, "Why did you start this company in the first place?" How would you tell that story?

Most companies have a version of their story already—it's the "about us" page of your website or the "company profile" description on your social media. When's the last time you looked at yours? Now that you've done the important work to Obsess over your ideal customer and Differentiate your brand, it's time to review your "about us" story and see how well it incorporates your North Star Vision, Mission, Core Values, and Ownable Whitespace. Or not. My bet: it's time to rewrite your story.

Finding Your Brand Voice

As you create your Unrivaled differentiation, your brand finds its "voice." The words, phrases, examples, and pace of speech that are particularly suited to you and your audience. I'm not talking here about what you say but how you say it. Think of your voice as your brand's personality. If your brand were a person, would you describe it as playful or serious? Energetic or careful? Rugged or refined? Creative or scientific? Surprising or reliable? Take some time to brainstorm on the words that best describe your company's personality. That personality must shine through when you tell your story.

Some of our favorite consumer brands are experts at using their "voice" to Differentiate themselves from their competitors. They can transform a shopping trip into a fantastic brand experience. Consider Trader Joe's. Why do they have obsessive loyalty from their customers? Because when you shop there, it's an immersive experience. They don't stock the same global brands you find at Stop & Shop or Publix. Shopping at Trader Joe's is almost like a treasure hunt. You discover new items, and you know they will taste great and not cost a fortune.

Now think of Trader Joe's unique personality. It's quirky and fun. It's direct and very personal. They bring their voice to life with handwritten signs, funny sayings, and tidbits of interesting information, all to engage their ideal customers. The "newsletter" at the front of the store has "stories" about the items on sale. It feels authentic, not glossy and fancy. Trader Joe's never talks down to their customers—they know their market is smart and savvy. Everyone working there engages with the customer, asks them how their day is going, and shares a bit about themselves. It's like talking to a friend, not a clerk. Even their titles are informal and fun: captain and first mate, not manager and assistant manager. Their voice is a key part of the brand experience that sets Trader Joe's completely apart from all other grocery stores (you don't really even think of it as a grocery store); they sound like a trusted friend who likes to have some fun. They are masterful at delivering a consistent, unique, customer-obsessed voice. They don't sound like Stop & Shop, Publix, or Whole Foods. Their voice differentiates their brand so they can stand out and apart.

The power of voice is just as important for B2B companies as it is for B2C companies. Especially in crowded markets or niches where it's tough to stand out, a consistent, unique brand voice creates a connection with your ideal customer and is a core part of your brand experience.

Think about Customer Relationship Management (CRM) software companies—a very crowded space that was dominated by Salesforce for many years but has attracted some aggressive competition. How does Salesforce maintain their Ownable Whitespace, and how do newcomers hope to succeed and grow? Differentiation is essential, and it comes through loud and clear in their voice.

Salesforce, as the largest and most established player in the market, has a strong, direct voice. They know they have a sophisticated enterprise executive audience. They speak their language and create a connection with that community. They also serve lots of brand-name clients, whom they mention often as a way to signal: if you are a serious player, we are the partner for you. Which is far different from upstart Apollo. Their voice is clearly geared to a different audience, and their personality is bold, with no reservations: "go for it." Their promise: "reach every buyer on earth." Their offer: "sign up free forever." No holds barred here—they understand their ideal customer is probably a smaller, scrappy company (just like them) that is ready to run into the fray.

Your positioning statement, story, and voice are all important elements of your Brand Manifesto—they are the *words* you use to stand out. But as the saying goes, a picture is worth a thousand words.

CHAPTER 18

THE POWER OF VISUAL IDENTITY

Remember our CEO from the book's introduction? He came to me with a simple request: "We need a new logo." The truth is, there was no way to know if they really needed a new logo or not. The only way to know was to start at the beginning and Obsess over their customers. The CEO was decisive, and once we completed the Voice of the Customer research, we learned that they weren't losing customers because of a logo. When we dug in, we discovered that the brand experience of their most valuable customers was the real problem, not the logo.

Your logo is a critical element of your brand's Visual Identity. Your Visual Identity is strategic. It's made up of very thoughtful, purposeful decisions about what your brand looks like and feels like to your ideal customer. When a logo is strategic, it becomes your company's calling card.

Unrivaled brands harness the power of Visual Identity. By doing the hard work you just finished (*Giddy Up!*), you can now align your Visual Identity to your Business Ethos and Ownable Whitespace. You are likely to see some areas of opportunity. Perhaps your logo needs a refresh. Or the images you use in your go-to-market need to evolve. These visible touchpoints create an emotional connection and positive brand impression that draws your ideal customers ever closer to you.

Unrivaled Businesses Make Visual Identity Strategic

Unrivaled businesses use their brand's Visual Identity to do some heavy lifting when it comes to brand experience and optimizing the marketing budget. Think of companies that do this really well.

Liberty Mutual uses an emu and a bright yellow background. When you see that color—and the funny emu—you think of them. T-Mobile, on the other hand, is hot pink. Notice how their ads include customers wearing hot pink shoes, holding a hot pink notebook, or ordering a hot pink cupcake. When you see a cell phone ad, you don't even need to see their name; all you need is the hot pink to tell you it's an ad for T-Mobile.

The same rules apply to B2B. It's why you can't help but think about HubSpot when you see digital ads and billboards around the city of Boston featuring their orange signature color.

This Visual Identity—the color palette, typography, logo, brand mark, imagery, and style elements—work together to connect with your ideal customer and make your brand memorable. An experienced designer or design team will help you ensure your Visual Identity strategically aligns with your Business Ethos and Ownable Whitespace to bring your brand to life for your ideal customer.

Your Visual Identity is a strategic system that helps you:

- Stand out from the competition.

- Connect with your target market.

- Convey your North Star Vision, Mission, Core Values, and Ownable Whitespace.

How does Visual Identity accomplish all that? Look at Airbnb. Founded in 2008, Airbnb's original logo was a blue, balloonish-script font. In 2014, they introduced a new logo font, along with a brand mark to align with their Unique Value Proposition (UVP): "belong anywhere."

The new logo is a visual expression of Airbnb's commitment to create a diverse and inclusive global community [Mission] where people can feel at home wherever they are [North Star Vision]. "This symbol of belonging, coined 'Bélo,' highlights Airbnb's message of standing for something much bigger than travel. Additionally, in line with color psychology, their logo uses a pink-red hue to convey a sense of love and nurture."[1]

Consistency Is the Holy Grail to Stand Out

Visual Identity goes beyond your logo to all the real-world manifestations of your brand and what it looks and feels like—across every channel in every interaction with your ideal customers. Your Brand Manifesto is the playbook that ensures all your Visual Identity decisions are consistent. Consistency is the holy grail, and Unrivaled companies are unwavering in using their brand to guide their Visual Identity.

According to Harvard University professor George Miller, it takes an average of seven impressions for a person to remember a company name or brand.[2] So you need to be sure that every touchpoint your market encounters consistently sends the same message. Your brand voice, your story, your positioning, your Visual Identity across your website, your ads, your social media, your trade show booth—all of it must be consistent for your ideal customer to remember your company.

Achieving brand consistency is key to being Unrivaled, and it's where lots of companies struggle. Sales gets out of sync with marketing. Outside agencies get out of sync with your Brand Manifesto. Suddenly, there are new messages and different visuals out in front of your ideal customers. It might feel repetitive to you to say the same thing, in the same way, over and over and over. But that's the point! You are building trust with your target market—they know you and remember you, so they can trust you.

Rely on your **Brand Manifesto**. It eliminates confusion in the marketplace and creates internal efficiency. It is the playbook that informs your entire go-to-market—every marketing plan, every advertising campaign, every sales pitch deck, and every touchpoint with your customers. It helps you create a consistent brand experience for your ideal customer. Follow your Brand Manifesto, and every customer and prospective customer will easily understand what you stand for, how you stand apart from the competition, and why you stand alone.

But perhaps the most important function of your Brand Manifesto is that it aligns your entire organization. Unrivaled companies use their Brand Manifesto to get everyone rowing in the same direction and championing the brand. This takes us to Step 3 of the Unrivaled Growth Framework.

Giddy Up!

DIFFERENTIATE

We've covered a lot of ground in Step 2, taking you through the process of differentiation by defining what you **stand for**, surfacing how you **stand apart** from the competition, and amplifying how you **stand out** as the unquestioned number one choice for your ideal customer. In this critical step of our Unrivaled Growth Framework, we've uncovered the following components to successfully Differentiate:

1. To stand alone, you must stand for something, stand apart from the competition, and stand out from the crowd in the eyes of your ideal customer.

2. Your Business Ethos explains what you stand for, including your North Star Vision for a better world, your Mission Statement that drives your entire company to make this Vision a reality, and your Core Values, which are the principles that guide all you do—values and beliefs that resonate with your ideal customer.

3. Through our unique approach to competitive analysis and self-scouting, you have identified the Ownable Whitespace where you stand apart from your competition (and which you express in a short and sweet UVP).

4. To stand out, you need to make sure all the customer-facing elements of your brand are aligned with your Business Ethos and Ownable Whitespace, including your positioning statement, voice, story, and Visual Identity—and put them all together in a playbook called your Brand Manifesto.

How Differentiated Is Your Company?

| 1 | 2 | 3 | 4 | 5 | 6 | 7 | 8 | 9 | 10 |

We do not stand out to our ideal customers because we're not clear on what we stand for or what makes us stand apart from our competition.

We have done some work on competitive analysis and have scouted out some of our unique values and benefits, but we haven't fully developed our Business Ethos or Ownable Whitespace.

We have clearly articulated our North Star Vision, Mission, Core Values, and UVP and are using differentiation as the Unrivaled competitive advantage to win the hearts and minds of our ideal customers and stand apart.

If you scored 1 through 4, start at the beginning of Step 2 and get to work now on articulating your Business Ethos and Ownable Whitespace so your ideal customers know what you stand for and how you stand apart from your competition. If you scored 5 through 8, focus on prioritizing and filling in the differentiation gaps and moving that score closer to a 9 or 10. If you scored a 9 or 10, *Giddy Up!* Keep up the great work! You're differentiated and standing alone—Unrivaled growth is within reach!

Quick Wins to Differentiate

To truly stand apart, you have to stand for something, stand apart from your competitors, and stand out from the crowd, all of which takes time and effort. But here are some things you can do right now to get a jump start on Unrivaled differentiation:

- Ask a few ideal customers to describe what you do and why it's different from your competitors. (Be sure to listen to the specific words they use!) Do they understand what you stand for?

- Rewrite your home page to include your UVP and positioning. Remove features and buzzwords and focus on your company's unique value and benefits for your ideal customer.

- Review your "story" against what your ideal customer cares about the most. Where are the opportunities to create more of an emotional connection and amplify what makes you different?

Unrivaled Growth Framework™

Five Steps to Achieving Explosive Business Growth

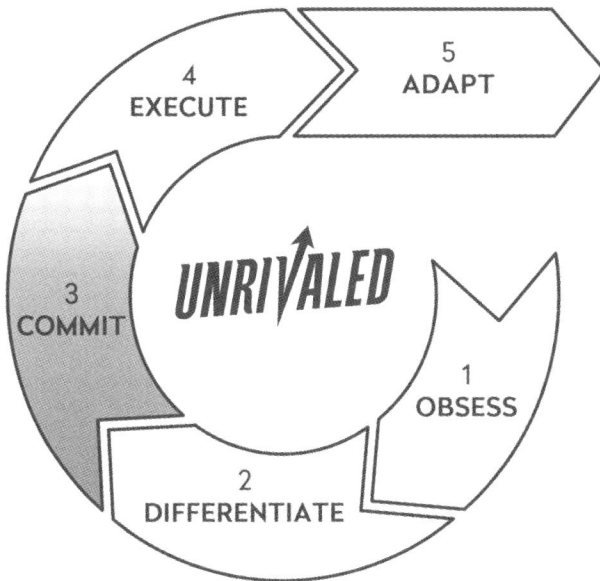

3 COMMIT
Get every member of your team rowing in the same direction and championing the brand.

STEP 3

COMMIT

"If you could get all the people in an organization rowing in the same direction, you could dominate any industry, in any market, against any competition, at any time."

—PATRICK LENCIONI, FROM HIS BESTSELLING BOOK,
THE FIVE DYSFUNCTIONS OF A TEAM

CHAPTER 19

GETTING YOUR ENTIRE TEAM ALIGNED

I was leading an Unrivaled workshop for a group of high-powered CEOs. As I was teaching the curriculum, the group was engaged and positive, soaking it all in through Steps 1 and 2. When we arrived here at Step 3 of the framework, one of the CEOs stopped and said, "This is the step that we can't seem to get right at my company." Other heads were nodding, and a spontaneous discussion began with the CEOs sharing their personal experiences about how tough it was to get the entire organization aligned and committed.

I'm not going to sugarcoat it. Step 3 in our Unrivaled Growth Framework is where most businesses fail to become Unrivaled. You've done the incredibly hard work of getting customer obsessed and differentiating your company. You've carved out your Ownable Whitespace, and you've created your Brand Manifesto. It's tempting to skip this mission-critical Step 3. Unrivaled companies are obsessed, differentiated, *and* committed! It's time to get everyone on board. To achieve explosive growth, your entire organization must be aligned with your brand.

Alignment of any type is no easy task. Keeping your body in alignment requires exercise, stretching, and movement. Keeping your business in alignment requires constantly living and championing your brand. To reach Unrivaled alignment, everyone in your organization must be committed to walking the talk—marketing, sales, service, product, customer success, operations, finance, IT—everyone. Without commitment, companies spin, circle, and churn like a rower out of alignment with the coxswain. Everyone must be rowing in the same direction and living your brand so the internal commitment maps to the external execution.

As I was writing this book, my daughter had an experience that perfectly illustrates the threat to a business that isn't committed and aligned. She was looking for a summer job during college. She decided to apply to a brand she loves. Not just loves, but has loved for many years. It's not an exaggeration (though it's not my favorite thing to admit!) that she has spent thousands of dollars on this well-known sports apparel brand's merchandise over the years. She's a superfan, their ideal customer—the bullseye of their target market.

Commit
Everyone Rowing in the Same Direction

The job was totally in her wheelhouse, and she was super passionate about the company and the opportunity. She applied online and got an email saying they'd be in touch to set up an interview. She was thrilled—imagine working for a brand that you're already a brand ambassador for!

Interview one, interview two, and then . . . they ghosted her. Radio silence. No emails, no phone calls, nothing. She tried to contact them, but she never received a response. And just like that, my daughter's impression of this brand was changed, and it called into question whether she wanted to purchase anything from them again.

I'm not saying they should have hired her (well, as her mom, of course I think any company would be lucky to hire her), but what shocked and frustrated both of us was that this behavior was so out of line with their brand. This company has built its brand on being supportive, empowering, and inclusive, especially of young women. But when it came to hiring, they did not walk the talk.

Now, you might say, well, that's different. They weren't treating her badly as a customer—she was just a job applicant. But consider the ripple effect. She feels let down and disrespected by a brand she loves. She tells people about this negative experience, and not only does she become unlikely to buy from them again, but this one experience changes the way we both feel about this brand. We both have been informal brand ambassadors of this company, buying, sharing, recommending, and proudly wearing their logo. The worst part? I guarantee we are not alone. A few voices—well, you might think they won't make a big difference. But problems like this get more pervasive. They creep into the market, and soon your brand is tarnished as a place people don't want to work.

Employees—both current and prospective—expect you to walk the talk. If you say you stand for something, it must come through in all of your interactions, both internally and externally. This company did not walk the talk during this interview process. A very quick email could have gone a long way to close the loop and leave both my daughter and I feeling like at least they lived up to their Business Ethos, even if the answer was, "I'm sorry it's not a good fit, and here's why." This lack of commitment to championing the brand soon turns into a misalignment with your customer and a breach of your moat—there are lots of other choices that suddenly emerge.

The damage can go far beyond alienating just one customer. Ninety-three percent of users read online reviews before making a purchase decision, and "86 percent say they would think twice about making a purchase from a company with bad reviews." Negative reviews spread like wildfire and can cost you both current and future customers. One study found that "a business can lose up to thirty customers just based on one bad review. Making up the deficit can take time and up to twelve new positive reviews to reduce the sting of the one bad review."[1]

As your business grows, you will not be able to oversee or participate in every brand experience your prospects and customers have. And you will not be able to monitor every single touchpoint a potential employee has with your company. The reality is you'll never know which part of your organization your ideal customers and prospective employees will encounter next. That's why it is mission-critical to make sure that every member of your team—every person in your organization, as well as outside agencies and partners—is on the same page, rowing in the same direction, aligned with your Business Ethos and Ownable Whitespace and **committed to the brand**.

Brand Manifesto: More than a Poster on the Wall

I remember going into one of my client's offices and seeing a framed poster of their Vision and Mission hanging on the wall. As I was leading a workshop with a group of midlevel managers, I asked, "So what does the company's Mission mean to you?" They all just kind of looked at me. "*Our Mission?* Oh, I can't remember what that is . . . It's got so many words . . . I think I saw it on a poster in the break room."

I love the idea of putting your commitment up on the wall. But unless every person in your organization champions the brand and knows their role in bringing it to life, those posters are just a bunch of words people pass by—instead of words that they connect to that inspire action.

True alignment takes relentless commitment and communication. It takes buy-in and reinforcement from the top, and it takes the same message everywhere you turn. True commitment happens when the North Star Vision and Mission infiltrate every department in your company and create a shared purpose. When they mean something to every person, they become part of the fabric of your entire organization. When everyone understands their role in achieving the North Star Vision and Mission and embodying the Core Values in everything they do—from interviewing a candidate to launching a campaign to building a new product feature—suddenly their work takes on new meaning, and they feel connected to something bigger than themselves.

Commitment creates a shared understanding of your brand from marketing and sales to customer service and operations to human resources and finance. Unrivaled companies get everyone walking the talk.

Unrivaled commitment won't come from just a poster on the wall. That's why Unrivaled companies use their **Brand Manifesto** to help everyone in their organization champion the brand. Even the best sales reps and the most creative marketing teams will underperform if they are not aligned with the brand. But when everyone is rowing in the same direction, you gain efficiency, effectiveness, and explosive growth.

Think of a symphony orchestra. Individually, you have great musicians—maybe someone is a really talented violinist and someone else is amazing at the oboe, the clarinet, the cello, or the tuba. (My husband learned how to play the tuba in high school!) But if they are not all playing the same music, it sounds awful. Unrivaled alignment happens when everyone is reading from the same music, playing in the same key at the same tempo, watching the conductor for cues, and listening to the other instruments around them. Only then can you make beautiful music—or, in your case, achieve Unrivaled growth.

Example of Core Values

Subaru's "Six Stars to Guide Us"

People Should Feel Love and Respect at Every Interaction with Subaru

★1

Make "Yes" Your North Star

Look for ways to serve and engage our customer and our communities.

★2

Be a Shining Example for Others

Demonstrate the highest integrity and trust.

★3

Provide Light in Darkness to Lead the Way

Provide solutions to problems, finding ways to make all stakeholders smile.

★4

"Be the Star" of Someone's Day

Be compassionate, empathetic, and an advocate for our customer, retailers, employees, and all stakeholders.

★5

Celebrate the Entire Constellation

Embrace diversity in people, ideas, and cultures.

★6

Shine Brighter, Every Day

Strive for speedy, continuous improvement.

2

Alignment Starts from Day One

Here's what happens when your team isn't fully aligned. Sales is off doing their thing. Marketing's off doing their thing. Customer service? They're off doing their thing too. Because everybody is rowing in a different direction, there is no unified understanding of the brand, and the boat isn't going anywhere.

Unrivaled companies understand that alignment with the brand starts from day one. For example, Subaru uses their Core Values in the hiring process and their first-day training.[3]

Make sure everyone in your company ecosystem is in lockstep with your brand. They all have responsibility for championing the brand at every turn, for delivering on what you stand for and walking the talk. In smaller companies, like early-stage start-ups where you have a small team, it can be easier to get everyone aligned as long as you make it a priority. In larger companies with thousands of employees, freelancers, agencies, partners, and satellite offices, getting everyone committed and aligned can be more challenging. Regardless of the size of your company, rallying your organization to champion your brand is where Unrivaled companies stand apart. Here we go. *Giddy Up!*

CHAPTER 20

RALLYING YOUR ORGANIZATION

So how do you get everyone on the same page? How do you make sure everyone understands, values, and uses the Brand Manifesto as their guide? Hanging a poster in the break room is great, but you can't simply rely on that. Just like printing up little cards with your North Star Vision, Mission, and Core Values is a nice reminder, but just handing them out to everybody and never mentioning them again doesn't work. There is no set it and forget it. You've got to rally the entire organization. Get every member of your team rowing in the same direction and championing the brand.

Your Brand Manifesto is the playbook to guide everyone on your team. To make sure it doesn't just gather dust on the shelf, Unrivaled companies are intentional and dedicated when it comes to educating and motivating their team to align with the brand. Particularly when you are introducing these elements for the first time, you need a launch plan.

Designing an Unrivaled Launch Plan

Figure out:

- *Who do we need to tell?* Answer: Everyone in your organizational ecosystem. This means you need a list so no one is forgotten or left out.

- *How do we reach everyone?* Answer: In some organizations, it's pretty straightforward because they're small and everybody's in the same location; for other organizations, there are people in the field or in other offices, maybe all over the world.

- *How do you get everybody together?* Answer: If it's possible for everyone to literally be in the same room together—do it. It's incredibly powerful. If that isn't feasible, you'll need a virtual meeting. The way we typically do that is with a town hall meeting, which includes every single employee around the world, wherever they are, piped into a live stream somewhere.

- *Who else, beyond our employees, needs to hear this?* Answer: Anyone who touches the brand. That might be outside consultants, agencies, strategic partners, designers, freelancers, or anybody who has a hand in helping communicate your brand. That includes board members and investors. I've been asked to present this work at my clients' board meetings. The Brand Manifesto always creates a strategic discussion and often unlocks new ideas and approaches that drive growth, profits, and the ultimate competitive advantage.

- *What do we need to tell them?* Answer: That we are uniting around a North Star Vision and driving toward a specific Mission. We are guided by Core Values. Our ideal customer is someone very specific and very special—here's what they look and sound like, what they care about, and how they make buying decisions. We occupy a very specific Ownable Whitespace where we give our ideal customer unique value and emotionally connected brand experiences they can't get anywhere else.

- *What about the Visual Identity?* Answer: Yes, that is important too. You will be unveiling your new Visual Identity—colors, logo, typography, imagery—and showing your entire company not only what it looks like but how to use it. Driving home consistency is key! If you're rebranding, that can be a big undertaking. There are lots of considerations when immediately changing every visual touchpoint across the entire company. You may need to communicate the new brand and explain that some things are going to be phased in. Something that really helps is a "cheat sheet" with your

North Star Vision, Mission, and Core Values. Something people can tack up on their board or next to their computer monitor so they don't forget. And creating new business cards and email signatures with the updated Visual Identity so people feel personally connected to it right away.

Launching with a Party

I love a good party. For one of my clients, I helped them create an Unrivaled launch plan that had both an internal and an external focus.

For the internal brand launch, we invited the entire company—from the guys in the field wearing hard hats and safety vests all the way to the guys in khakis and button-downs in the office at headquarters. Everybody was together, we had refreshments, and the new Visual Identity was on banners, napkins, balloons, and swag. The CEO got up to rally the three-hundred-plus people in the room. He shared why the company was rebranding and what it meant to him personally and for each person at the company. He talked about how the rebrand would carry this forty-year-old family-run company into the future as the Unrivaled market leader and would create commitment, excitement, and camaraderie.

Soon after the internal launch, we had the external launch. It was the company's fortieth anniversary, and we took advantage of this big milestone to unveil the new brand and celebrate with customers, prospects, partners, press, and other key stakeholders. It was a beautiful evening at a museum in Boston and a perfect way to share the new brand with everyone in their ecosystem.

And while you might not have the budget for a big launch party, don't discount the value of a celebration to communicate your new brand elements and rally support for your company. Generating excitement and connection to your brand creates sustainable business growth, and there are lots of different ways to celebrate this exciting milestone for your company.

Brand Starts at the Top

In most organizations, marketing is the owner of the brand. In Unrivaled companies, brand is the CEO's job. Not to say that marketing, sales, and other executives are not involved, but the brand starts at the top. If you want real buy-in—Unrivaled commitment to your brand—the CEO or president has to get up in front of the entire organization and say, "Team, this is nonnegotiable. This is who we are. This is how we're changing. This is how we will win. This is not just a marketing campaign. It's not just a sales tactic. It's a 360-degree commitment to living our brand, and you are instrumental in making it happen and walking the talk. Here's why it's so important to you regardless of which department you work in."

Why Brand Is So Misunderstood

Oftentimes when CEOs hear the word "brand," they tune out. Many CEOs perceive brand to be "fluff"—devoid of measurable business value or ROI. They often think of a brand as just a logo or color palette, an ad campaign, or a decision about the color of business cards.

Brand is the real-world manifestation of your business in your market. It's what your ideal prospects and customers interact with every day and fall in love with. Brand is strategic. It creates an emotional connection with your bullseye so that you can stand alone as their Unrivaled choice. It is the tailwind for explosive growth, making it easier and more cost-efficient for you to attract and retain the most valuable customers for your business. Brand is not just a rallying cry for your entire organization; it is the force multiplier for Unrivaled growth.

That's why brand is the CEO's job. It doesn't mean that marketing and other departments don't have an important role in your company's brand. It means that brand has to start at the top. Many executives and teams I work with are frustrated with trying to "push the brand up." It typically doesn't work. Business leaders and other team members are important stakeholders and are instrumental to the success of this brand work. But the CEO needs to be driving the bus. Brand is a growth strategy that starts at the top.

There is a popular misconception that only B2C companies need a brand. While many B2C companies spend millions on competitive brand differentiation, B2B companies have been late to the game. Most of the time when B2B companies bring me in to help them with a growth problem, they have not done the work that you are doing here—to stand for something and stand apart from your competitors. B2B markets are incredibly crowded—look at supersaturated markets like cybersecurity, biotech, health care, and financial services—everyone in the market is vying for the same ideal customer. What will make them choose you? Your brand makes your company the obvious choice.

Weaving Brand into the Fabric of Your Organization

Your new brand elements must become part of the fabric of the company across every department and everything you do. You have to walk the talk. How, exactly, that happens is different for every company, but here are some tips for success:

- Use your Brand Manifesto as part of the hiring process. Naturally, a viable candidate must have the necessary skills and experience for the job. But don't stop there. Ask questions that are tied to your Core Values. Assess how candidates respond—are their values aligned with your values and vice versa? Do they seem animated and engaged by your North Star Vision and Mission? Do your Core Values align with the candidate's personal goals? These guardrails can help you choose the right employees who will thrive and help your company thrive.

- You can also use your Brand Manifesto as part of your performance reviews. Team members can be reviewed on how they live up to your Business Ethos. For one client, we created team "spotlight" awards that were given to employees who lived the Core Values. They created an award for each Core Value and delivered them quarterly at the company town hall meeting. Other clients have created quarterly goals based on a Core Value to focus on each quarter, moving toward a measurable goal.

- Celebrate and reward team members who excel at living in the customer mindset. Your ideal customer persona is part of your Brand Manifesto—and Unrivaled growth comes from obsessing over that persona consistently. Make sure each member of your team is aligned and committed to the ideal customers you serve.

- Tie company performance and results to your Business Ethos and your Ownable Whitespace. Whenever you're talking about company performance—whether at a company meeting, a media interview, a shareholder meeting, a TED Talk, or a cocktail party— make a point of relating P&L results to your Business Ethos and how you Differentiate to stand apart as the Unrivaled market leader.

In all these ways, your Brand Manifesto shifts from being just a document to becoming the playbook for success that rallies every member of your organization.

CHAPTER 21

EVERYONE IS A BRAND AMBASSADOR

Every single person in your company is a champion of the brand. They may not think of themselves that way. A software engineer may not think of themselves as a brand ambassador, but they go to cocktail parties, baseball games, and PTA meetings. They go to networking events and conferences. When someone says, "What do you do?" if they say, "Well, we're a software company that has XYZ technology and ABC features," so what? But if they say, "We help our customers deliver more projects faster," they've said something memorable and distinctive. And when you have thirty people who all say the same thing at thirty cocktail parties or networking events throughout your marketplace, that's powerful. Imagine the impact when it's three hundred people or even thirty thousand people!

It can be tempting to focus your brand ambassador efforts more on the people in your company who are "front of the house"—such as sales, customer service, and customer success. But be sure not to overlook the people who might be more "back of the house"—employees who have important roles but might not interact directly with your ideal customer on a day-to-day basis, such as marketing, operations, engineering, HR, finance, or product development. They all play key roles in championing the brand and bringing your brand to life for your ideal customer, even if they might not interact directly with them regularly.

Brand Ambassadors

Every team member champions the brand

Why Sous Chef Sue Loves Her Shoes

Imagine someone in a warehouse, picking something from the shelf and putting it in a box for a customer. Does it make a difference to them if they can envision that customer and understand them in 3D? Heck yes! When everyone in your company can shift from seeing a faceless human who ordered something to seeing the ideal customer persona in 3D, new opportunities to connect come to life.

For our warehouse employee, imagine they can now see the ideal customer persona, Sous Chef Sue. She works long hours on her feet and needs shoes that are both comfortable and stylish. She is a loyal customer who purchases from companies that care about what's important to her. All of a sudden, your warehouse employee can understand their role in helping Sous Chef Sue love the brand and her shoes.

When I come in to help companies get their organization excited about and committed to their brand, I often hear things like: "I'm just a back-office person. I don't have anything to do with the customer" or "I work in the warehouse filling orders, and I'm not on the front lines with the customers." Many "back of the house" employees are doing critical day-to-day work, but oftentimes their job feels disconnected from the customer, and it can be hard to see the impact they have on growth. People want to be part of something bigger than running marketing campaigns, picking items off shelves, coding software, or paying invoices. The more you can connect their work to the ideal customer and your Business Ethos, the more fulfilling and rewarding their jobs become. Even when they are standing at a conveyor belt, putting shoes in a box.

With a new understanding of the ideal customer and the company's Business Ethos, our warehouse employee came up with an idea. "You know, Sous Chef Sue would love it if we put a little note in the box for her. It would remind her why she decided to buy from us and also make her smile after a long day on her feet." Ideas can come from anywhere in the organization, and we can all share in how to delight and surprise our customers. When everyone has a role in that, regardless of their job in the organization, your company is propelled to Unrivaled status.

Hammer, Glue Gun, or Plunger?
Unrivaled Companies Know

When your entire team is aligned and committed, customer obsession becomes part of everyday life. This level of commitment to your brand shifts conversations from subjective to objective. Instead of building what we might like, we build what our ideal customer persona wants and needs the most. It aligns your entire organization and directs your focus squarely where it belongs: on your ideal customer bullseye. The result is no wasted motion, increased collaboration, and customer-driven solutions—all of which lead to explosive growth.

I speak from experience. My kids were little, and one night, the toilet broke. The handle wasn't working, and the toilet wouldn't flush. The water was rising. Stuff was swirling. I was trying not to panic as I imagined what would happen if the water spilled over the side. It was *not* a fun moment. My son came in with a hammer. I searched for a plunger. My daughter brought her glue gun. One problem—three different solutions.

When we approach a problem, we bring our experiences and perspectives to the table. Our first instinct can be to solve it "our way." But the real question is: What does your ideal customer want? Are you giving them a glue gun when they really need a plunger? Unrivaled companies know what their ideal customers need and what they care about the most. They stay in lockstep on the entire journey. Every person in the company becomes a brand ambassador, someone who truly champions the brand. They win the hearts and minds of their ideal customers and increase lifetime value. (And in case you're interested in the ending to the toilet story, the solution was a YouTube video and a very kind neighbor who helped me replace the "flapper valve.")

A More Efficient Way to Grow

Unrivaled companies benefit from aligning, committing, and prioritizing. They ask themselves questions like, "We're doing all these things, but are these the things that our ideal customer persona wants from us? Maybe we can forget that new feature or style—it doesn't matter to Sous Chef Sue. She doesn't care about fussy buckles and straps or the latest fashion trends. She just wants an easy-to-put-on shoe with lots of cushion that looks good and gives her the comfort she needs for a long shift on her feet." All of a sudden, a new efficiency play begins to happen at a rapid pace where you can stop or avoid doing things that your ideal customer doesn't care about! Instead, you can start doing the things that are important to them—things that will move the needle. You have a different way to prioritize everything you do.

In addition, by empowering and aligning your team to be committed to the brand, you encourage customer obsession—a new customer-centricity—that can power better decision-making, more efficient product development, more effective marketing campaigns, more impactful sales efforts, and more. Once you've mastered commitment, your go-to-market is ready to be supercharged in both efficiency and effectiveness. That's when all efforts unify to propel you to Unrivaled growth. ***Giddy Up!***

KEY LEARNINGS
FOR STEP 3
COMMIT

Often Step 3 is the most challenging step for companies to conquer. But it's an essential part of the Unrivaled Growth Framework. The key learnings from this important step are:

1. True commitment requires consistent communication and reinforcement.

2. Your Brand Manifesto aligns your organization and creates a consistent brand experience.

3. Brand is strategic and starts at the top.

4. Rally your entire organization with a launch plan.

5. Celebrate your brand and weave it into the fabric of everything you do—walk the talk.

6. Everyone in your organization has the potential to champion the brand and be a brand ambassador.

Looking at your company today, how well are different parts of your organization aligned with your Business Ethos? Is everyone rowing in the same direction toward your North Star Vision? Could most people in your company explain what your brand stands for?

How Committed Are You?

○ ○ ○ ○ ○ ○ ○ ○ ○ ○
1   2   3   4   5   6   7   8   9   10

Our organization lacks commitment to our brand.	Some people are on board and committed, but not everyone is walking the talk.	Our entire company is rowing in the same direction, and every member of the team is a brand ambassador championing the brand on a daily basis.

If you scored a 1 through 4, get to work now on committing to your brand from the top down. At a score of 5, you still have some work to do! Remember: when you are championing the brand every day and reinforcing it with your team, that is when you consistently win! If you scored a 6 through 8, you are on your way—look for ways to deepen the brand's emotional connection with everyone in your organization to empower and align people toward your North Star Vision. A 9 or 10? *Giddy Up!* Use your Brand Manifesto to reinforce your commitment and champion the brand.

Quick Wins to Commit

I know this step can be tricky to implement, but there are several things you can put in place immediately that can help you Commit at an Unrivaled level:

- Record a "rallying cry" video to send to all employees.

- Write an all-company email to communicate key points from your Brand Manifesto.

- Create a branded screen saver or Zoom background for all employees.

- Align job descriptions and performance reviews with brand Core Values.

- Review company hiring practices and job descriptions and align them with your brand.

With your entire team aligned and living the brand, you're ready to Execute! **Giddy Up!**

Unrivaled Growth Framework™

Five Steps to Achieving Explosive Business Growth

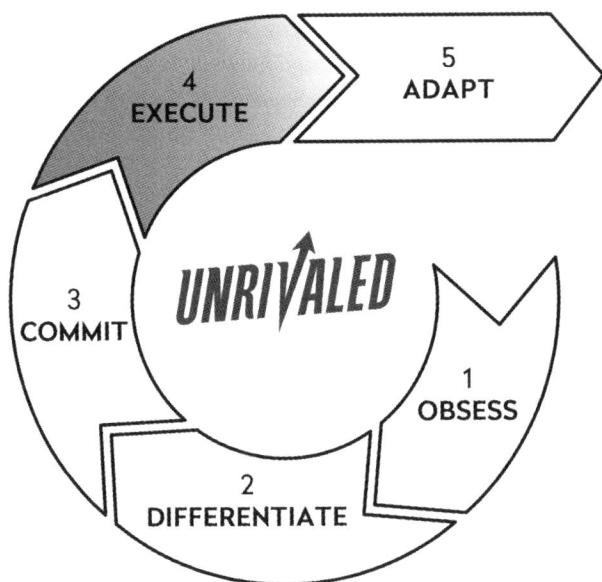

4 EXECUTE
Create Surround Sound go-to-market activities to achieve explosive business growth. Giddy Up!

STEP 4

EXECUTE

"As much as I love tech and live tech and dream tech . . . it's the killer go-to-market that always wins."

—VIJAY PANDE, VENTURE CAPITALIST AND GENERAL PARTNER AT ANDREESSEN HOROWITZ

CHAPTER 22

ARE YOU PROVIDING A SMOOTH LANDING OR A BUMPY RIDE?

I flew two different airlines in two days. Same price. Same weather. Same travel clothes. Two wildly different brand experiences.

The first leg was JetBlue. Snacks and drinks for all. Super friendly staff. Inclusive, premium feeling.

Then I flew American Airlines. I was late to my gate with no time to grab food or water. So I got on board and took my seat. I saw them up in first class starting to take drink orders and thought, "Thank God, we are next!" I just needed some water to rinse down a half-eaten granola bar I'd found in my bag. They have to at least serve us water, right?

Then, *whoosh*, the curtain closed. No drinks for you!

I immediately knew where I stood. Sure, I expect first class to offer a different level of service, but when I compared my economy experience on American Airlines to my economy experience on JetBlue, they were two wildly different brand experiences. Suddenly I didn't feel like American Airlines's ideal customer. Their ideal customer was on the other side of the curtain. That little curtain was a record-scratch moment—a brand experience failure that had me looking for the exit.

Every brand experience is a customer experience. A recent study found that companies earning $1 billion annually can expect, on average, an additional $700 million by improving customer experience. For SaaS companies in particular, excellent customer experience can translate into increasing revenue by $1 billion. That's because 86 percent of buyers are willing to pay more for a great customer experience. Oftentimes, bad customer experience is a silent killer—research shows that only one in twenty-six dissatisfied customers actually complain. The rest simply stop doing business with you.[1]

Seeing Your Go-to-Market Through Your Ideal Customer's Eyes

Think of your ideal customer. They interact with your company through all the go-to-market activities and campaigns you deploy across lots of different channels. Even if they don't walk into your office or talk with you on the phone, there are countless touchpoints that affect how they think about you. They might hear your product or service advertised on a podcast. Or see your name on social media. Your company might come up in a Google search or appear in a banner ad. They might log in to your platform, receive an email, hear your name from a colleague, or simply see your logo at a trade show. Every element of your go-to-market creates a brand impression. Create a good impression, and you're building Customer Lifetime Value (CLV) and loyalty. Create a bad impression, and you're sending them off to your competition.

When Tony Hsieh founded Zappos®, their Unique Value Proposition (UVP) was "delivering happiness." This powerful UVP translated into every experience with their brand. I experienced this happiness on many occasions as I interacted with Zappos—every touchpoint made a difference as a customer and created feelings of joy, excitement, and gratitude. Brand experience goes beyond the sale. It consistently reinforces your UVP and Business Ethos across every channel and at every turn to shape your ideal customer's experience and leave a lasting impression.

Executing with Emotion

When it comes to your go-to-market, every time your ideal customer interacts with you, they experience your brand, and you want them to feel: "This is the company for me—they know me, they understand me, they care about me, they *get* me."

Nike is a brand that has perfected using their go-to-market to create an emotional connection with their ideal customers. Their Business Ethos and everything they stand for come through in the way they Execute. In 2007, Nike made a strategic decision to point their arrow at the female athlete market, and they hired Lauren Fleshman to star in a series of ads for their first-ever female running shoe. Fleshman was a highly decorated runner who'd won five NCAA titles and two national championships. Nike came up with a campaign that pretty much copied a campaign they'd done with soccer star Brandi Chastain (a wildly successful campaign, I might add). When Fleshman read the script, she said no. Look, she explained, I'm not a sex symbol. I'm an athlete. If you want to "objectify" me, let me show who I really am.

Nike listened. The new script went like this: "Look at me. Study me. Understand me. I am not a small pink version of a man. Don't give me small pink versions of a man's running shoe. I'm Lauren Fleshman. I'm a runner. And I'm a woman."[2]

Imagine young female athletes all over the world hearing that through Nike's go-to-market. Do you think they trusted that Nike understood them and would make a shoe meant just for them? You bet they did.

Nike knows what their brand stands for, and Fleshman reminded them to stay true to their North Star Vision and Mission of inspiring young female athletes. (Remember, we're *all* athletes to Nike!) By following their Business Ethos to develop a campaign that their ideal customer immediately identified with, they created an emotional connection that is far more powerful than mere features and benefits. Tapping those neural pathways of emotion is the best way to transform your messaging from uninspiring to Unrivaled.

When you consider all the individual activities that make up your go-to-market—from advertising to social media to sales calls to product demos—are they creating a positive brand experience? When your ideal customer hears your name, what do they feel? Do they think of your company as the number one choice to solve their problems? Do they recognize you as distinct from the competition? Is your brand the snowplow out ahead making it easier for your customers to choose you?

Unrivaled companies create a positive brand experience with every element of their go-to-market. Now let me show you how to Execute your go-to-market so you can become Unrivaled too.

CHAPTER 23

HOW TO EXECUTE AN UNRIVALED GO-TO-MARKET

I just bought a bag of grapes. They looked pretty good—plump, juicy, not too squishy. Then I spotted a QR code on the bag. It said, "See the full story behind this product."

To be honest, as I lined up my camera to snap the code, I was thinking: *What kind of stories do grapes have?* And then, *bam.* The grapes wrapped me in a delicious vine of brand.

Divine Flavor—a brand I had never heard of—was suddenly brought to life. They weren't selling me grapes. They were making an emotional connection. Their Mission: "It is our promise to provide Better Food for a Better World."[1]

Unrivaled brands like Divine Flavor know that a great marketing campaign isn't about grapes. It's about sharing your values, beliefs, and purpose with the people who want and need you the most. Divine Flavor made an impact on me. Their clever use of a QR code created a juicy impression. I am no longer just buying any bag of grapes. I'm looking for their brand.

What Does an Unrivaled Go-to-Market Look Like?

Unrivaled go-to-market execution drives powerful growth—in sales customers, loyalty, and profits. I'm about to show you how to Execute your go-to-market so well it takes your ideal customer from prospect to raving fan, efficiently and effectively.

When I say "go-to-market," I'm talking about everything you do to attract, win, keep, and grow your ideal customers. We're talking acquisition, engagement, and retention—the specific channels, tactics, and activities where you invest your time, resources, and budget to attract and retain your ideal customers. Email marketing, content, thought leadership, events, PR, SEO, SEM, product demos, YouTube videos, trade journal interviews, TED Talks, trade shows, digital ads, billboards, direct mail, social media posts—all the marketing campaigns, sales activities, and messaging you deploy make up your go-to-market.

A successful go-to-market:

- Aligns your marketing, sales, product, success, and service teams.

- Uses your Brand Manifesto consistently.

- Creates shared goals, metrics, and KPIs.

- Delivers personalized, relevant, memorable brand experiences.

- Builds advocacy, affinity, and loyalty.

- Solidifies differentiation.

- Generates efficiency.

- Drives sustainable growth.

In other words, your go-to-market is the lifeblood of sustainable business growth. It's everything you do to attract and influence your prospects along their journey, plus the continued experience you deliver that delights customers and ignites loyalty and lifetime value. A successful go-to-market takes maximum advantage of every step of your ideal customer's buyer's journey. Let's take a closer look at that journey now.

CHAPTER 24

THE TRANSFORMATION OF THE BUYER'S JOURNEY

While QR codes, like the one I found on my Divine Flavor grapes, have been around for years, until recently they simply were not part of the traditional "buyer's journey." Maybe you saw a Welch's grape juice ad on TV or saw a BOGO special at the grocery store. Buying a bag of grapes meant going to the produce section, popping a grape in your mouth when no one was watching (just to make sure they were good), and heading to the checkout line.

But the buying experience has been transformed. The way people buy things today is fundamentally different from the way it used to be. In fact, it has changed so dramatically and continues to change so rapidly that "the way we've always done it" just doesn't work. Technology is evolving, your ideal customer's wants and needs are evolving, and markets are evolving. Right now, by reading this book, you are evolving! Your knowledge and perceptions are evolving as you open your mind. You are soaking in new ideas. You are gaining new insights that will put your business on a new path. You know that doing things the same old way is not going to work in reaching your ever-changing customers and achieving your audacious business goals. *Giddy Up!*

Whether you're selling a five-dollar bag of grapes or $50,000 enterprise software, your customer's buying decision is now a 360-degree experience. Your prospects and customers are surrounded by sales and marketing messages coming at them from all directions, all channels, all the time. Bombarded by so much information and persuasion, buyers easily get confused, distracted, overwhelmed, and exhausted, making it harder than ever to convince them to choose your products and services.

But what if the buying experience wasn't a bombardment of noise and instead it was a beautiful symphony in Surround Sound? What if your ideal customer, the prospect who sits at the very center of your bullseye, was swept along their journey so smoothly that, by the time they made their decision to buy, they couldn't wait to choose you and only you?

To accomplish that, you must *understand their journey*—from casual window shopping to signing on the dotted line—and then *surround them with brand experiences* that all point to you. Unrivaled businesses know their customers so well that they meet them where they are, anticipate what they need along the way, and make it efficient and enjoyable to go from awareness to consideration to decision.

The Shifting Buyer's Journey: From Highway to Maze

Most business leaders understand that the buying decision is a journey, with several steps buyers take during the decision process. What many don't fully understand, however, is that the buyer's journey is not a straight line—it weaves and winds around from online ad to website, to the product page, to customer reviews, to social media posts, back to website, to the pricing page, over to competitors' websites to compare, do additional research, then request a demo, then back to reviews and FAQs, then to pricing again, now maybe ready to make a decision, but oh wait, there are more decision-makers, so we go back to pricing and website, over to procurement, and three, six, or nine months later, they purchase! B2C and B2B buyers have different journeys in terms of inter-actions, channels, and experiences, but the complexity is often still the same. And every buyer might have a side road or detour that makes their journey just a little different. Customer-obsessed companies live in their ideal customer's mindset. They are empathetic to their buyer's decision-making steps and understand that the journey looks more like a maze than a highway.

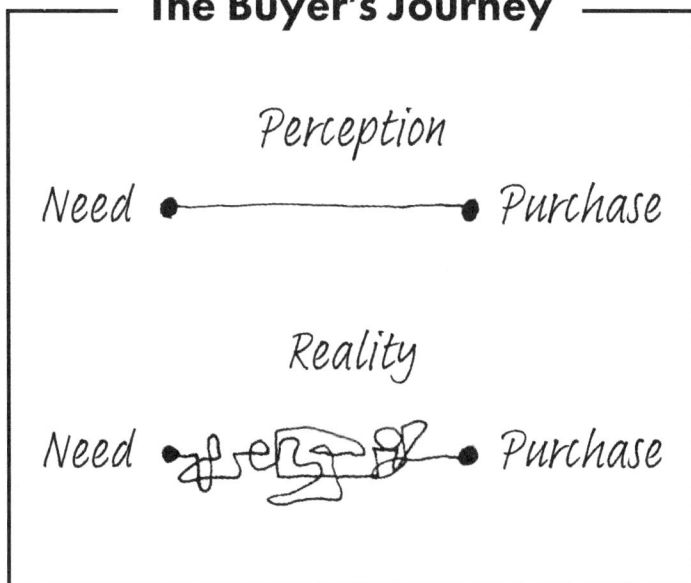

The Buyer's Journey

Perception

Need •————————• Purchase

Reality

Need •〰〰〰〰〰〰• Purchase

Take, for example, how people used to buy a car: decide which type of car you want to buy, set your budget, walk into the showroom, test-drive a car, negotiate a deal, go to a second dealer to see if you can get a better price, then buy a car.

How people buy a car today: start looking around at cars on the road, consider what you need, ask family members or friends, check CARFAX®, look at websites, read reviews, check out social media accounts, watch a YouTube video, go to the dealership or do a virtual test-drive, search for the best price, go back to read reviews again in more detail, do online research, talk to owners of that type of car, go back to the dealer (or never even set foot in a dealership!), negotiate, then buy a car.

Today's buyer's journey is a winding road made up of millions of touchpoints. Every experience a customer or potential customer has with your brand is a touchpoint along that journey—from the first time they hear your name until well after they have purchased your product or service.

Gartner does a great job of illustrating this reality for B2B firms (and the same principle applies to B2C!).

B2B Buying Journey

Illustrative

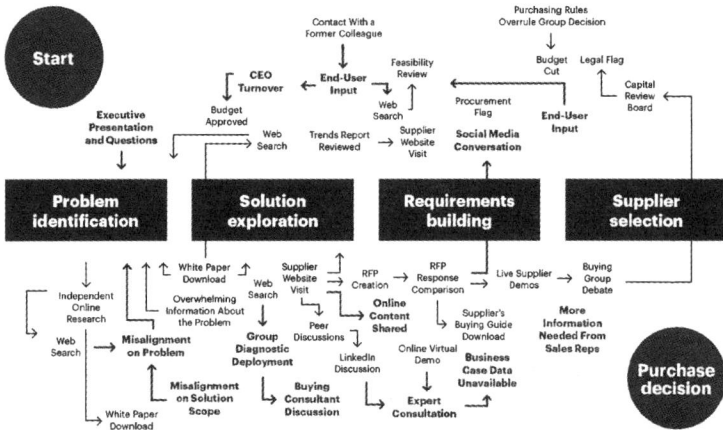

Start

Executive Presentation and Questions

Problem identification · Solution exploration · Requirements building · Supplier selection

CEO Turnover · Budget Approved · Web Search · Trends Report Reviewed · Supplier Website Visit · Web Search · Feasibility Review · End-User Input · Contact With a Former Colleague · Procurement Flag · Social Media Conversation · Budget Cut · End-User Input · Purchasing Rules Overrule Group Decision · Legal Flag · Capital Review Board

Independent Online Research · Web Search · Misalignment on Problem · White Paper Download · Overwhelming Information About the Problem · Group Diagnostic Deployment · Misalignment on Solution Scope · White Paper Download · Web Search · Supplier Website Visit · Peer Discussions · Buying Consultant Discussion · LinkedIn Discussion · RFP Creation · Online Content Shared · RFP Response Comparison · Supplier's Buying Guide Download · Online Virtual Demo · Business Case Data Unavailable · Expert Consultation · Live Supplier Demos · Buying Group Debate · More Information Needed From Sales Reps

Purchase decision

Dead Ends and Distractions

Let's break down the maze a bit to better understand the buyer's mindset, steps, and considerations. Go-to-market campaigns are designed to take prospects from the top left (start) to the bottom right (purchase decision). Along the way, there are some key milestones—problem identification, solution exploration, requirements-building, and supplier selection. After that, it gets hairy. As your ideal customer identifies their problem, they search the web, read white papers, do online research, and more—which might cause them to rethink the scope of the problem or simply to become overwhelmed with information. Meanwhile, a key executive raises a new problem, or the CFO sets new budget goals, further clouding milestone number one. Once the problem is identified, your future buyer moves on to solution exploration—as you can see, that presents another raft of questions, rabbit holes, and dead ends. As does building the RFP and selecting the supplier (you) they ultimately want to do business with.

Instead of a linear journey, the buyer's journey is a maze in which your prospect often takes two steps forward and one step back, can hit a dead end, and then has to go back or around. Even when they think they've moved on to the next milestone, something can cause them to go back and reconsider or revise what they want and need.

You can envision a similar journey for B2C customers—the potential customer identifies a problem, explores solutions, researches different products, checks pricing, defines what they need or want in the solution, compares brands, reads reviews, rethinks what they need or want, narrows their consideration set, reads FAQs, reads specs, rereads reviews, asks friends, adds to cart, lets product sit in cart, thinks about purchase, does a bit more research, watches reels and YouTube videos, and then finally clicks purchase. "Add to cart" and "click to purchase" are not as linear as we think.

It gets even more complicated when you realize that before they buy, your ideal customer seeks out info, often *a lot* of info, about your company from places that you can't control, see, or track. "Dark social" was the term first used by Alexis C. Madrigal, a journalist and former editor of the *Atlantic*. It is "the act of content being shared through private means which can't be tracked by analytics tools or software."[2] Imagine your buyers consuming content, reading reviews, and searching for information across "dark social" to get the information they need to make a decision. By the time they get to signing a contract, they've read a competitor's blog post, chatted with your customers on Reddit, talked to buyers of your product via DMs, and gotten referrals behind the scenes. This organic sharing is not all trackable buyer's journey stuff, but it's all happening.

"It's estimated that up to 84 percent of all online sharing activity occurs through dark social, making it a digital marketing phenomenon that requires in-depth understanding and strategic utilization."[3]

Bottom line: the access to information, the explosion of shareable content, and the maze of the buyer's journey can make it really hard for companies to get their go-to-market right.

CHAPTER 25

MAPPING YOUR BUYER'S JOURNEY

Thanks to Steps 1, 2, and 3 of our Unrivaled Growth Framework, you already have most of what you need to anticipate your ideal customer's buyer's journey. Refer back to the customer-obsessed work you did in Step 1 of our Unrivaled Growth Framework. What did your existing customers tell you about how they decided to buy from you? Channel your ideal customer persona. (*What matters most to CFO Charlie as he starts his buyer's journey? Would he start by checking out online reviews or asking a colleague in the field?*) Put yourself in your ideal customer's shoes and imagine how they move from "start to finish"—from prospect to customer. Remember, this isn't about how *you* buy or what *you* like. It's about your ideal customer and building the personalized experiences that *they* want and need, where *they* want and need them, and when *they* want and need them.

Between talking to your ideal customer persona and working together with your sales team, your customer service and success teams, your marketing team, and your product team, you've got the intel you need to map out the buyer's journey for your ideal customer.

When I work with my clients to map out the buyer's journey, we typically gather in a room with a whiteboard and lots of sticky notes and markers or we use a remote collaboration tool. We lay out all the steps the customer takes to make a decision. We analyze prospect, customer, and go-to-market data. Here are some of the questions we answer together.

- **Where do ideal customers come from?** What channels drive your most valuable customers? Why do they use those channels? When do they use those channels? How do the channels work together across the buyer's journey?

- **Where does your ideal customer get information they can trust?** As we've seen, buyers today have access to endless information, but what sources do they rely on? When they are serious about spending money to solve their problem, where do they turn for research, advice, and solutions? Consider your ideal customer's trusted sources. Trade journals? Industry events? PR? Referrals from colleagues? Podcast interviews? Social media? Review sites? And remember, it may be *all of the above*—and likely more! Today's buyer's journey is a multichannel experience.

- **How did customers first hear of you?** It might be some combination of the list above, but how did you *initially* get on their radar? You need to be in the decision set to land the contract. A Bain & Company study surveyed B2B buyer behavior and found that 80 to 90 percent of respondents have a set of vendors in mind before they do any research, and just as important, 90 percent of them will ultimately choose a vendor from the day-one list.[1] The day-one list is the trust list. If your ideal customer doesn't know you exist, you won't even get invited to the RFP. Brand awareness gives you a seat at the table.

- **Who are the decision-makers?** Different people will hop on the train at different points in this buyer's journey, and you have to be prepared to show, tell, and prove to each one of them that you are the right choice. The "executive sponsor" or "champion" of the project might be the economic buyer, but chances are they are not the only voice in the decision. This is especially true for B2B sales. Imagine an HR tech software sale. You're pitching your product to the chief human resources officer (CHRO), but you're also selling to the director of HR, the HR staff, the CTO, and the CFO. Most companies in this example just focus on the CHRO.

But there's a full "buying committee" of influencers who can affect the choice of which software to buy. You've got to understand their roles in the initial *and* ongoing sale. For a B2C company, the "buying committee" might be a family like mine where the teenager "decides to buy" the product but the parent is technically the economic buyer. Knowing these types of buyers in the purchase decision will help you speak to their specific hopes, needs, questions, fears, and concerns along the way.

- **Why don't people buy?** Knowing why they *don't* buy is almost more important than knowing why they do. When you understand objections, you can overcome them. I conducted a go-to-market workshop with one of my clients recently. When I looked at the data around objections, I noticed some patterns. When we discussed it as a team, we quickly realized that the objections were actually things our ideal customer wanted to know but didn't, so it turned into an objection. We turned the objection into an opportunity to educate the ideal customer and almost immediately turned a pain point into a specific brand experience that kept the buyer moving forward in the sales process, improving pipeline velocity.

Mapping out the typical journey that your ideal customer takes from start to sale gives you a clear picture of how they reach their buying decision. It also equips your business with new information and new ways to connect with your ideal customer to make sure their buyer's journey leads to you.

CHAPTER 26

KNOWING WHAT TO START, STOP, AND OPTIMIZE

To transform your business from underperforming to Unrivaled, your go-to-market must match up with the buyer's journey of your ideal customers.

When I do this work with my clients, we often start with an inventory of all your go-to-market activities. Now map that to your ideal customer's buyer's journey. Ask yourself:

- What go-to-market touchpoints are we missing?

- Do we have the right experience for the ideal customer at each touchpoint?

- What go-to-market activities are wasted motion?

Stop every activity you're currently doing that doesn't show up on your ideal customer's buyer's journey. Start every step on the buyer's journey that isn't in your audit. And for every step remaining, optimize it. Before you buy the next ad, design the next landing page, sponsor the next event, build the next e-book, or create the next sales pitch, stop, drop, and check your buyer's journey!

One of my clients, a private equity–backed company, was spending a significant part of their marketing budget on events and trade shows. As we were doing the buyer's journey work together, we uncovered an important piece of data. When we looked at where their ideal customers came from, we noticed they were coming from some of the smaller events, but nothing was coming from larger events, where we were spending the most. There was no ROI from the bigger events. How could that be? Our new knowledge about the ideal customer revealed that they were not at these trade shows. They merely sent a member of their team, while the senior executives were attending smaller, more intimate events where they could learn from their peers and collaborate in a more hands-on way. Our ideal customer was on a different journey. This important insight redirected the budget to more personal events and generated more qualified leads that drove more revenue.

Maximizing Your Go-to-Market Dollars

Businesses regularly waste millions of dollars every year on marketing and messaging that their ideal customers never see. So, our first wave of transforming your go-to-market is to start and stop. Be where your ideal customers are and cut out the rest.

Just because "everyone" is on a specific social media platform doesn't mean that's where your ads and messages belong. One of my clients called me and said, "We need to be on Instagram!" I started asking why. I pulled up the ideal customer persona and started reviewing it, when the CMO said, "I am not sure our ideal customer even has an Instagram account." The company avoided wasting precious budget on a new channel, and instead we laser-focused on where the ideal customer was getting their information. Wasting money where your target market is not is like opening the windows during a cold Boston winter and just letting all the expensive warm air float out. Your go-to-market is an investment. Before you invest in a channel, ask these questions:

- Is this channel where my ideal customer does their research on how to make the right buying decision?
- Is it where they get advice?
- Is it a trusted source?
- Is it where buyers are buying?
- Do we have the budget to be successful in this channel?

Don't waste time and money going down the wrong road. And the budget question is super important. Make sure you have the expertise (aka people) and discretionary spending to be successful in the channel. I've seen lots of companies spread the budget too thin. When you know the buyer's journey, you can meet your ideal customer where they are.

On the flip side, are you ghosting your prospects at some point in their journey? If you are not present at every step of the journey, you are likely missing a connection point and leaving the door wide open for your competition. If they rely on LinkedIn to discover products like yours, how will you show up there and stand out? If they rely on trade shows to discover new software, what shows are a "must-do" for your business? If they rely on white papers to inform their decision-making process, what topics should you cover and where should you promote them to get in front of your target market? This is your chance to fill any gaps in your go-to-market strategy.

Optimize Every Touchpoint

Once you "start and stop," you have a new streamlined buyer's journey— no more wasted steps and no missed steps. Yet even if you are showing up in all the right places, are those campaigns and activities producing leads who convert into buyers? Unrivaled brands optimize every touchpoint on that buyer's journey to make sure each one translates into sales.

Most go-to-market teams have the data to know at a high level what's working or not. Going a few clicks down to see buying patterns and surface intent gives us new information to add to the buyer's journey. You might see that certain content, channels, experiences, and interactions are more efficient in getting the ideal customer in the door.

The best way to optimize every touchpoint and to fix go-to-market activities that are not giving you the ROI you want is to refer back to your Brand Manifesto as the ultimate guide. Look at each step or activity on your streamlined buyer's journey through the following lens:

1. **Customer Obsession**: Take out your ideal customer persona. Are your go-to-market activities targeted to your ideal customer? Are you speaking their language, solving their problems, in a voice that resonates with them? *In other words, is your go-to-market obsessed*

with your ideal customer? When I talk to clients about go-to-market, they instantly think of all the marketing campaigns they've deployed. And we spend a lot of time analyzing those campaigns to figure out what's working and not working—and why. Time and time again, the biggest reason go-to-market campaigns don't work is because they are not aligned with what the ideal customer needs, wants, and cares about the most. They might be clever, they might be funny, they might have super high production values. But if they don't connect with your ideal customer, they are not going to deliver ROI and will end up wasting precious budget. Targeting everyone targets no one.

2. **Ownable Whitespace**: Review your messaging against your Ownable Whitespace, UVP, and positioning. Does it clearly communicate the unique way you can solve your ideal customer's problem—better or differently from all your competitors? Does it use the words that matter most to your ideal customer?

3. **Lean into Your Business Ethos**: Engage your ideal customer in your North Star Vision, Mission, and Core Values. Create the emotional connection that makes it easier to choose you—this is your chance to bond a customer to you for life by explaining not just what you can do for them but why you do it. Customers choose businesses who share their values and beliefs. Make sure your go-to-market helps your ideal customer understand what drives your company so you can build an emotional connection that transcends price and features.

4. **Stay On-Brand**: To truly supercharge your go-to-market, every message and experience must consistently reinforce the brand. That includes your voice, your story, and all the Visual Identity work you did to make your competitive differentiation come to life. Use your Brand Manifesto to drive all these marketing, sales, and messaging efforts. Don't be tempted to stray from your identity! People need to hear something seven times before they remember it. Repetition and consistency are your go-to-market friends.

Is Your Influencer Taking You Off-Brand?

One of the sneaky ways to stray off-brand is when companies partner with an influencer to speak to their target market. Decades before social media turned "influencer" into a marketing buzzword, brands were already spending millions of dollars on influencers with celebrity endorsements. Almost every famous athlete you can think of has an endorsement deal for insurance, sportswear, fast food, you name it. Celebrity influencers drive instant recognition—and an instant connection to a product or service—as long as the brand and the athlete appeal to the same target market.

If a celebrity influencer is well-known for racing around in hot sports cars, don't ask them to promote a minivan. If a celebrity draws millions of teenagers to rave concerts, don't ask them to promote health insurance for seniors. And what happens when your celebrity influencer gets arrested or has a messy divorce? Suddenly their affiliation with your brand might be costing you millions.

In 2022, $16.4 billion was spent on influencer marketing—and two-thirds of brands and retailers said they intended to increase their influencer spending in 2023. In fact, 23 percent of these businesses intended to designate more than 40 percent of their marketing budget to influencer marketing. Fortunately, research shows that businesses are also taking a wiser approach to how they spend those billions of dollars. "Rather than selecting the most buzzworthy influencer or celebrity, businesses are seeking to partner with creators who share their values, with the goal of forging a more genuine connection between the brand, influencer, and audience."[1] Bottom line: for Unrivaled execution of your go-to-market, make sure it perfectly aligns with your Business Ethos and your ideal customer.

Start, stop, and optimize can transform your go-to-market. You will cut out wasted time and money, seize every opportunity to connect with your target market, and ensure that every sales activity and marketing expense carries your prospects smoothly and effortlessly toward choosing you.

Based on your ideal customer's journey:

What gaps do you need to fill?

_____

_____

What channels and activities do you need to stop?

_____

_____

What activities can you optimize?

_____

_____

CHAPTER 27

THE POWER OF SURROUND SOUND

Throughout the buyer's journey, your target market will experience your go-to-market in a variety of ways. And it might be tempting to "change it up" with different messages for different channels and media. After all, won't your market get bored with the same message over and over and over again? While some variation makes sense, such as shorter, more informal language on social media versus more detail in a product demo, the greater risk comes when you send out competing messages that just amount to a lot of noise.

Unrivaled companies know that the single most effective way to optimize their go-to-market is by employing a technique I call **Surround Sound**.

When I was at J.P. Morgan, I was fortunate enough to work with some incredibly smart people. We were young, energetic, and ambitious. Together, we covered a lot of ground.

There were two other executives who were my peers, and together, we were a force. We were constantly thinking of what we could do better: for our customers, for the business, and for shareholder value. We had a way of uniting. More voices equals more clout.

The three of us worked in marketing, and we had a seat at the table, but J.P. Morgan was going through a major transition, and there were lots of decisions happening cross-functionally at levels well above ours.

One day, we had a big idea. We decided to approach our boss's boss (do this at your own peril!) to pitch them and get their buy-in. Halfway through the meeting, the executive stopped us. "Wow, you guys are like Surround Sound!" We were in lockstep, consistently communicating our idea. I was pitching it from a brand experience perspective, explaining how it could add value to our ideal customer. My colleague on the right was talking all about the competitive positioning and how our idea gave us an advantage. My colleague on the left drove the customer retention angle and how our idea would skyrocket customer affinity and loyalty.

We were conveying our message from all sides. In stereo. The executive couldn't escape it. We sold him on our big idea because we were in lockstep, all three of us reinforcing the same message. He would see us coming and say, "Here comes Surround Sound!"

That's how your customers need to experience your brand—in Surround Sound from all angles. That immersive experience we have in a theater when the sound is all around you. No matter what the source—your website, ads, emails, social media, salespeople, customer service team—customers need to hear your Unique Value Proposition (UVP) over and over and over. Just like Surround Sound, your sales reps might provide the deep bass while your paid ads provide the hi-fi treble, but it all works together—powerfully and efficiently—to communicate a unified message, leading your buyer to a single conclusion: this is the number one choice for me. Surround Sound meets your ideal customer where they are and envelops them in your brand—from the message, to the Visual Identity, to the experiences, to your consistently differentiated value— *they can't not see you*!

Unrivaled Execution
Surround Sound Experiences

Living in a Barbie World

I grew up obsessed with Barbie.

The special travel case, the Dreamhouse, the camper van, the sports car, the equestrian set, the beauty salon—I had it all. My friends all had Barbies. We had Barbie parties. We played Barbie for hours. Sure, that was a hot second ago (I mean, not *that* long ago!). But think about this:

The Barbie brand launched in 1959, and sixty-plus years later, the Barbie brand is stronger than ever. Barbie is a billion-dollar brand, making up a third of Mattel's revenue.

When the Barbie movie came out in 2023, their brand campaign was a perfect case study in Surround Sound. In addition to all the regular marketing and promotion that goes into launching a major film, this brand went full Surround Sound. Barbie pink was everywhere—from billboards across the country to marketing campaigns by Gap®, Forever 21, Ulta®, and more. Barbie partnered with everyone from Bloomingdale's to Burger King®.

And it wasn't just Barbie-pink fashion trends and Barbie-themed burger toys. Warner Bros. cross-promoted the Barbie movie with a reality series on HGTV, *Barbie Dreamhouse Challenge*, coproduced by Mattel Television. A float promoting the film was featured in the 2023 WeHo Pride Parade in Los Angeles. You could even rent a real-life Barbie Dreamhouse in Malibu through Airbnb.

The target market for Barbie (both the brand and the movie) was wrapped in a pink cloud of impressions and experiences that translated directly to the bottom line. Mattel reported a 9 percent year-over-year increase in sales for the third quarter of 2023, including a 27 percent jump in doll sales. The company estimates that the overall revenue boost from the Barbie movie was close to $125 million, including sales of dolls, related merchandise, and movie earnings.[1]

By surrounding their target market with consistent reminders of the Barbie brand, this sixty-year-old brand's go-to-market was truly Unrivaled.

CHAPTER 28

UNRIVALED GO-TO-MARKET BUILDS RELATIONSHIPS

The goal of your go-to-market is, of course, to grow your business by making sales. But you can't walk up to a stranger and expect them to hand you thousands of dollars on the spot. First, you have to earn their trust and prove you offer something of value. They have to be comfortable with you and develop an emotional connection that makes it easy to choose you. In other words, Unrivaled go-to-market is designed to build relationships.

There is a natural progression to healthy relationships—in life and in business. You start with awareness and move to understanding and trust.

Forget about forcing people to act when they're not ready or throwing a bunch of spaghetti at the wall hoping for a quick fix. You've got to warm up your ideal customers—lead them to the sale on their terms. Make sure they understand you, which leads to trusting you, which leads to believing you. And it all starts with seeing you—otherwise known as *brand awareness*.

Most of my clients want to get the flywheel going, but without awareness, the flywheel can't fly. Instead of customer acquisition being a smooth, predictable process, it's rough and inefficient. Unrivaled companies know that brand awareness is the grease in the flywheel.

Unrivaled Go-to-Market

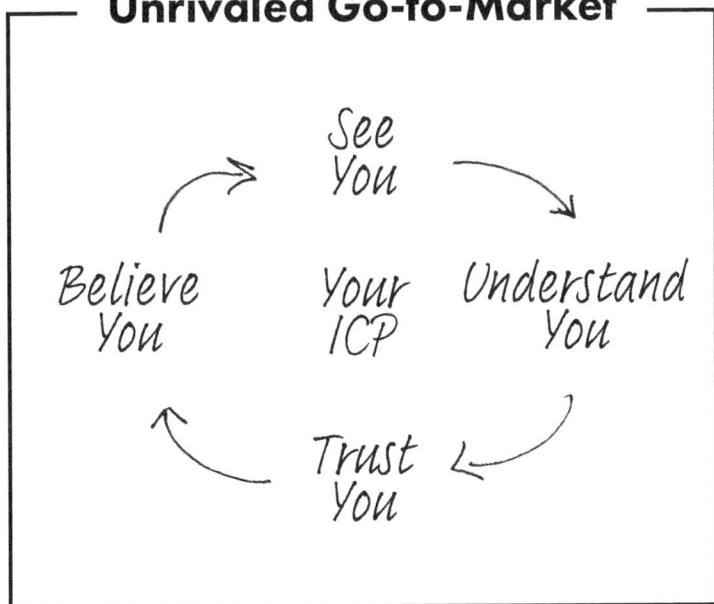

See
You

Believe
You

Your
ICP

Understand
You

Trust
You

The Lack-of-Awareness Problem

Many companies are plagued by a lack-of-awareness problem. A Fortune 500 client described the problem to me as: "If I'm talking to someone in New England, maybe they have heard of our brand, but most of the time our ideal customers don't know who we are."

We have seen that our ideal customer's buyer's journey moves from, as Gartner put it, "problem identification" to "supplier selection." But to be selected, you first have to be part of the decision set. The trouble is, they can't put you in the decision set if they are not aware that you exist.

Awareness is the fuel that turbocharges your entire go-to-market strategy.

"A study found that consumers are 2.5 times more likely to choose a brand they recognize over a lesser-known competitor" and "64 percent of consumers consider brand reputation and awareness when deciding which products to purchase." Brand awareness is the gift that keeps on giving and keeps you growing efficiently as the market leader.

Too many businesses skip the brand awareness work because they want to get right to the selling—and then they wonder why their go-to-market doesn't work. When customers are searching for a solution to a problem or desire, the easiest thing to do is choose a brand they already know.

B2B companies often struggle with creating brand awareness. Imagine trying to sell $50,000-a-year enterprise software to someone who has never heard of you. It burns through your capital and disenfranchises your team.

The explosion of media and information sources makes it even harder to achieve brand awareness. There is so much noise in the marketplace that buyers get overwhelmed and retreat to familiar ground.

At this point, you're not trying to close the sale—you're not even trying to convince them to download a demo or schedule a sales call. You want your ideal customer to *see* you. Establish your name as a trusted expert in your field. Your Brand Manifesto gives you the words. Put them to work in the right places, where your target market is gathering information, staying on top of the industry, learning new skills, and exploring new products and solutions.

Let's say your Unique Value Proposition (UVP) is "taking the headaches out of business travel." That's your Ownable Whitespace. All of your marketing campaigns ladder up to that promise. Maybe you produce video content explaining the new challenges of business travel. Maybe you produce a free report on the ten biggest mistakes business travelers make. Maybe you run a series of podcast ads with funny stories about business travel gone wrong. All your content and messaging are consistent with your UVP and help your ideal customers educate themselves to save time and money. And you're creating Surround Sound—the right channels where they are. It's all helpful and value-driven content—you're not pushing the trial, demo, or sale. You create trust with your ideal customers.

Regardless of what you're selling, people buy from people they trust. Part of your go-to-market's job is to create "trusted awareness," where your ideal customer gets consistent value from interacting with your brand—it's not just you trying to sell me something. Instead, your go-to-market creates relationships that lead to higher conversion rates, higher customer loyalty, and higher margins. Like all great relationships, Unrivaled go-to-market is built on trust.

Trust Drives Revenue

Sometimes I need a change of scenery. While I was writing this book, I decided to pack up for a few days and spend some time with my parents. On my drive, the "check engine" light flashed on. All I could think was, "Seriously? *Now*?" I had so many other things to deal with and no time to get it checked out. When I arrived at my parents' house, I mentioned it to my dad, who pragmatically replied, "Never mess around with a check engine light. You need to get that looked at right away." Before I could respond, he said, "I'll take it to Rands."

For decades, my family has entrusted Rands Automotive with the care of our cars. My mom drives past at least five other gas stations and over to the next town to fill up the car with gas at Rands. Their unwavering honesty, transparency, and quality service have earned our trust. They're not in the business of selling gas, parts, and service—they're in the business of people and building trusted relationships with customers like my dad. And it's this trust that fuels revenue for Rands.

Most business leaders I work with understand the value of trust— of course you want your customers to trust you. You want them to feel confident and secure about working with your company. But when the demands of product development, hiring, and technology start to pile up, worrying about trust goes out the window.

Trust, however, is one of the best investments any business can make. The simple fact is that *trust drives revenue*. It causes more people to spend more money with you more often.

- Better Conversion: According to a survey by Edelman, 81 percent of respondents cite trust as "a major consideration for brand purchase." Higher trust translates directly into closing more leads, driving more sales.[1]

- Higher Profits: According to Harvard Law research, "91 percent of business executives agree (including 50 percent who strongly agree) that their ability to earn and maintain trust improves the bottom line."[2] Companies with high levels of trust are more profitable—think of what this means to a business like Rands—or to yours!

- Beat the Competition: People with high brand trust (75 percent) will only buy products from that brand, even when the product isn't the cheapest, and would immediately consider buying new products from that brand without considering a competitor.[3]

- More Customers: Trustworthy businesses like Rands thrive on word-of-mouth referrals. Satisfied customers, confident in Rands's reliability, readily refer friends and family, generating invaluable referral revenue. Nielsen's research affirms that 92 percent of consumers trust recommendations from people they know.[4]

- Sustainable Growth: Trust goes beyond driving immediate revenue—it also builds a foundation for long-term success. According to Salesforce, "95 percent of customers say that if they trust a company, they're more likely to be loyal patrons."[5] This highlights the crucial role trust plays in scaling growth.

Buying Is Risky Business

The B2B buying decision is risky. A recent Gartner study showed that 77 percent of buyers say their last purchase was very complex or difficult. Combine that complexity with the number of vendors and products swirling around your target market, and the decision process becomes laden with risk.[6]

Your ideal customer is thinking: I don't have all the data to prove this is a good decision. What if I buy this B2B product and it's a disaster? The onboarding sucks, implementation is a complicated mess, training is little to none, and the service or customer success team is too busy to take our calls. Or, worse yet, the product doesn't deliver the value I was told it would and I can't prove the ROI.

The stakes for your ideal customer are *high*.

Our job is to reduce the risk for the buyer, which greases the skids for the sale. Trust de-risks purchase decisions by removing the fear of making a bad decision and creating confidence that your company is the best choice—the number one choice.

Yamini Rangan, CEO of HubSpot, knows the key role that trust plays in fueling HubSpot's success. She says, "Trust is the most important thing for your customer and your partner ecosystem. The goal is to inspire customers to move beyond being passive users and instead become enthusiastic promoters. Everything we did was aimed at growing trust. Ultimately, what's good for the customer is also good for the company."

Founded in Boston by Brian Halligan and Dharmesh Shah, HubSpot's product is Customer Relationship Management (CRM) software. But instead of talking about technology and features like AI, machine learning, and reporting, HubSpot talks about growing better together. They wrap their ideal customers in helpful, insightful content and experiences. They empathize with the tough jobs their ideal customers have, as they are often understaffed and underbudgeted marketing teams. By always focusing on "what's good for the customer," HubSpot has earned their ideal customer's trust and carved out a powerful Ownable Whitespace in the crowded SaaS field.

CHAPTER 29

THE GIFT OF CUSTOMER LIFETIME VALUE FOR UNRIVALED BRANDS

Most businesses focus all their sales and marketing efforts on acquiring customers—right now. But a successful go-to-market doesn't end there. Unrivaled companies know that profit margins soar when Customer Lifetime Value (CLV) climbs.

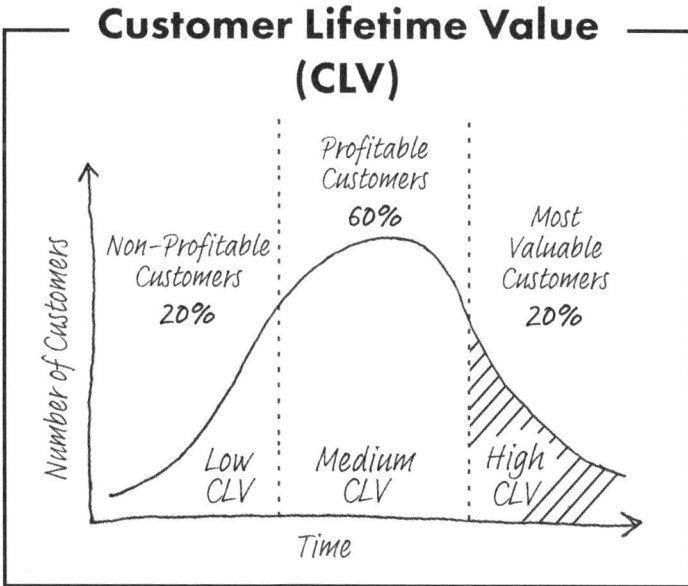

Customer Lifetime Value (CLV)

Non-Profitable Customers 20%

Profitable Customers 60%

Most Valuable Customers 20%

Number of Customers

Low CLV · Medium CLV · High CLV

Time

CLV is the net profit contribution of a customer to your company over time. It's another way of thinking about ROI—and making sure you get the most bang for every single buck. According to research by the Wharton School's Professor of Marketing David Reibstein, the probability of selling to an existing customer is up to fourteen times higher than the likelihood of selling to a new customer.[1]

Think of it this way: Let's say your Customer Acquisition Cost (CAC) is $1,000. If your net profit per sale is over $1,000, you're doing okay. But if that new customer only buys once, you're scraping just to stay above water. If that customer becomes a repeat customer, however, your ROI soars. In fact, if your customer spends $10,000 over the next three years, you're in high CLV territory, and it gets easier to reinvest profits back into your go-to-market.

Unrivaled companies achieve a double benefit when it comes to CLV. By dramatically streamlining your go-to-market activities, you can reduce your CAC, and by following our framework, you can also increase the amount of revenue you will get from each customer over time. Costs go down, revenue goes up—that sounds like a recipe for Unrivaled growth.

It all depends on keeping the most valuable customers and making it obvious that you're their best choice over and over. It starts the day you win a new customer and continues through the whole life cycle of your customer's relationship with you.

In many ways, the "post-purchase" experience is even more important than your acquisition strategies. After all the hard work and money you've spent to acquire a customer, the only way to maximize that investment is to *keep* that customer long-term. It's costly—and discouraging—to let them leak out of the bucket (remember the Leaky Bucket syndrome?) and have to constantly refill it. It's smarter and more efficient to reinforce that purchase decision, engage existing customers with great content and experiences, and make sure they love your product (or find out why if they don't). Doing so creates brand advocates (Seth Godin calls them "sneezers") and loyal fans who are just as obsessed with you as you are with them.

Benefits of CLV

→ Decreases customer aquisition costs (CAC) over time

→ Improves ROI

→ Increases profitability

→ Identifies customer retention gaps + opportunities

→ Defines GTM impact

Research shows that it's much easier (read: less costly *and* less difficult) to sell to your existing customers than to new ones. In fact, "the probability of successfully selling products" is 60 to 70 percent for loyal customers versus 5 to 20 percent for new prospects. Yet only 32 percent of executives cite customer retention as a priority. Consider this:

- Increasing customer retention by 2 percent lowers costs by as much as 10 percent.

- Profit can increase between 25 to 95 percent just by increasing customer retention by 5 percent.

- Loyal customers spend 33 percent more than new prospects.

- Loyal customers are five times more likely to repurchase, five times more likely to forgive, four times more likely to refer, and seven times more likely to try a new offering.[2]

No wonder Unrivaled companies invest time and resources on customer retention, dedicating their attention to turning first-time buyers into repeat customers and turning happy customers into loyal fans and brand ambassadors. When customers feel you know them and care about them, they tend to spend more and spend more often. When they become brand ambassadors, their support translates into positive word-of-mouth. That's invaluable promotional power—for free!

Maximize CLV

CLV soars for Unrivaled brands by thinking about the post-purchase customer experience in four stages:

1. Onboarding: Validation and reassurance.

2. Engagement: Regular communication.

3. Trust: Consistency and Core Values.

4. Loyalty: Raving fans and brand ambassadors.

The work you've done on differentiation and team alignment bears amazing fruit when it comes to CLV. As soon as you win a new customer, wrap them in a warm blanket of North Star Vision, Mission, and Core Values (onboarding). Share with them why you exist, the better life you envision for them, the better world you envision for everyone, and the Core Values that guide everything you do. Reassure them by repeating the promise of your Unique Value Proposition (UVP) and positioning—this is why they chose you; now validate that this is what they'll get.

Set up a plan to communicate regularly with your customers (engagement). Share news about the company that might help them be even better served in the future, and share news about the people inside the company to build rapport. Use the same voice that you developed in your Brand Manifesto—the same voice you've used in every communication since the very start of their journey.

And make them feel at home by consistently using the Visual Identity they saw when they first "met" you (trust). Make sure your customer support team is walking the talk aligned with the Brand Manifesto. Every time a customer hears from you, that consistent branding will say, "This is from someone I know and trust." It's like getting a postcard with familiar handwriting on it. When you see a message from someone you trust and respect, you read that first.

In all these ways, you are saying, "We are partners together on this journey. I know you, and you know me. We trust each other to help us both be more successful, more efficient, and more effective. And we share a Vision for how the world can be a better place for all of us." This is how Unrivaled companies build loyalty, turning customers into raving fans.

One more essential reality of CLV: you are *always* in "awareness and consideration" mode with your customers. They live out there in the real world where all your sales and marketing messages are deployed. Even after they choose to become a customer, they will still encounter the same brand impressions that new prospects do. If those impressions confirm the warm and happy feeling they have as a customer, you stay Unrivaled. If those impressions conflict with their feeling about your brand, market share can disappear overnight. You have to work every day to earn their mindshare and wallet share.

Companies spend hundreds or sometimes thousands of dollars to acquire a customer. Conventional thinking says that the higher your CLV, the more you can afford to spend on acquiring a new customer. But when you are Unrivaled, your go-to-market is so perfectly aligned with your Brand Manifesto and so perfectly in step with the buyer's journey that CAC costs actually *go down* while CLV soars.

CHAPTER 30

THE INCREDIBLE BENEFITS OF UNRIVALED EXECUTION

When you apply the Unrivaled Growth Framework to all your execution, you dramatically improve your current go-to-market strategies, cut out wasted efforts that are burning cash without providing any real results, and add new tactics that create a Surround Sound buyer's journey that sets you apart from the competition.

As Dharmesh Shah, founder and CTO of HubSpot, likes to say, "The more advocates you have, the fewer ads you have to buy."[1]

When you truly reach Unrivaled status, you discover a world of efficiency, effectiveness, and ROI on your go-to-market activities that leaves your competitors in the dust. Complex decisions are much simpler, and tricky choices are much more obvious. In addition, you can leapfrog competitors by avoiding wasted time and effort. When you stop doing all the things that cost money but yield no discernible ROI, you free your entire team to drive revenue and business growth.

The difference between Unrivaled and everyone else is *how* you Execute. It's sort of like grocery shopping—when it's time to go shopping, there are two types of people: people who make a list and only buy what's on the list, and people who go to the store and buy what they think they need and what strikes their fancy as they walk up and down the aisles. That's the discipline that Unrivaled companies have when they go to market. Marketing campaigns are laser-focused on the ideal customer. Messaging across all channels is consistent and brimming with benefits. Social media, the company website, and customer service all speak with the same voice and envelop customers in the company's Core Values.

Unrivaled companies don't just throw spaghetti against the wall to see what sticks. They don't throw money at the latest fad. The go-to-market activities of Unrivaled companies are not driven by what their competitors are doing; they are driven by a differentiated brand experience—applied to the ideal customer's specific buyer's journey—that puts every single decision into perfect focus.

Think about some of the Unrivaled companies we've talked about in this book: HubSpot, Subaru, YETI, Trader Joe's, JetBlue, Warby Parker, and Nike. Some of these companies have been around for generations, but not all. What they all have in common is a laser focus on obsessing over their ideal customer, carving out an Ownable Whitespace, committing to aligning their team, championing the brand, executing a consistent go-to-market in Surround Sound, and generating incredible customer loyalty. Oh, and one more thing they all have in common: significant financial success. HubSpot: achieved over $1 billion in Average Recurring Revenue (ARR) and one hundred thousand paying customers.[2] Subaru: profits up 196 percent in a single year.[3] YETI: net sales up $600 million over five years.[4] Trader Joe's: average revenue-per-square-foot that's double their competitors.[5] JetBlue: realized a 7.5 percent increase in revenue passengers, which generated $9.6 billion in 2023 operating revenue, an increase of $457 million.[6] Warby Parker: average revenue per customer up 9.2 percent in a single year.[7] Nike: gross profit from $12 billion to $22 billion over ten years.[8] That's what it means to be Unrivaled.

EXECUTE

Step 4 in our Unrivaled Growth Framework is where you meet your ideal customer in the real world. It's where you take everything you know about your ideal customer, everything you believe from your Business Ethos, everything that makes you stand alone in your Ownable Whitespace, and you Execute. To be Unrivaled in your go-to-market activities, you must:

1. Understand your ideal customer's buyer's journey. Map it out so you know how they make their buying decisions and what stops they make along the way so you can meet them where they are and keep them moving along.

2. Decide what to start and stop to maximize your marketing dollars. Don't waste time on messages that will never reach your ideal customers. Fish where the fish are. Do a go-to-market audit to be sure your go-to-market messages are in all the right places.

3. Optimize every touchpoint. Even if you are in "all the right places," are your go-to-market efforts yielding maximum ROI? Use your Brand Manifesto to make every single step on your ideal customer's buyer's journey lead to you. Repetition and consistency make your dollars go further and create the emotional connections that turn prospects into customers—and customers into fans.

4. Go-to-market extends to your current customers too. Unrivaled companies skyrocket Customer Lifetime Value (CLV) by creating trust and nurturing the four stages of customer retention.

If you scored a 1 through 4, your go-to-market execution will be more efficient and effective when you put your Brand Manifesto to work and define your ideal customer's buyer's journey. At a score of 5, you still have some

How Are You Doing?

O	O	O	O	O	O	O	O	O	O
1	2	3	4	5	6	7	8	9	10

Our go-to-market execution does not consistently follow our Brand Manifesto, and we do not know our ideal customer's buyer's journey.

We have done some work to define our buyer's journey but have not optimized our go-to-market or created Surround Sound.

We are running a successful go-to-market that is aligned with our Brand Manifesto, creating Surround Sound, efficiently generating high CLV, and driving sustainable business growth.

work to do! Focus on optimizing your go-to-market and creating Surround Sound to meet your ideal customer where they are—in stereo! If you scored a 6 through 8, your go-to-market is on its way to being Unrivaled—nice work. Use your buyer's journey work to find ways to fine-tune your go-to-market activities and brand experiences. At a 9 or 10? *Giddy Up!* Take full advantage of your Unrivaled go-to-market to drive CLV and sustainable business growth.

Quick Wins to Execute

As you work toward Unrivaled execution—with all your go-to-market strategies conducted in Surround Sound—here are a few immediate moves you can implement right now:

- Assess the last go-to-market campaign your company activated by looking at the campaign activities through the eyes of your ideal customer. Identify any changes you would make to align it to your ideal customer and run it again!

- Choose one of your social media channels and review the last five posts against your Business Ethos. Rewrite one of the posts and incorporate what you stand for to tap into the emotional connection of your brand, then launch it and test the results.

- Review your sales pitch deck to ensure your brand messaging is being articulated consistently in the sales process.

- Conduct a Surround Sound brainstorming session with your go-to-market team (include stakeholders from sales, marketing, revenue, customer experience, customer success, and so on) to create at least one new way to meet your ideal customer where they are.

- Add the question "Where did you hear about us?" to every prospective customer conversation and interaction (form fills, order confirmations, thank-you emails, and more).

Unrivaled Growth Framework™

Five Steps to Achieving Explosive Business Growth

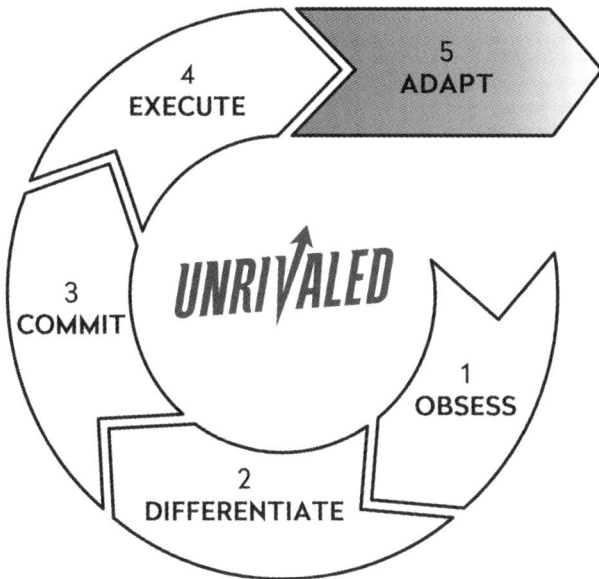

4
EXECUTE

5
ADAPT

3
COMMIT

UNRIVALED

1
OBSESS

2
DIFFERENTIATE

5 ADAPT
Grow with your customers
and stay Unrivaled.

STEP 5

ADAPT

"The measure of intelligence is the ability to change."

—ALBERT EINSTEIN

CHAPTER 31

TO BE UNRIVALED,
YOU MUST
STAY UNRIVALED

I was a new mom, up all night with a newborn. I spent many nights in front of the TV, flipping through endless channels at two a.m. I quickly got tired of infomercials and home shopping channels. I didn't have time to go to my neighborhood video store to pace around looking for movies to rent, and most of the time the titles I wanted were already checked out. It was a hassle, combined with needing to remember when to bring the videos back to avoid the late fees. I needed a better solution. I heard about a movie delivery service called Netflix from a friend. Within minutes, I had created a queue. Within days, DVD-formatted movies encased in little red jackets arrived at my door.

It changed everything for me. I couldn't wait to see the envelope in my mailbox! What my sleep-deprived brain couldn't imagine was how it was forever changing the home video industry. Behind the scenes, Blockbuster was under siege. A classic David versus Goliath story was unfolding. Until Netflix came along, Blockbuster was Unrivaled as the king of home video rentals. Sure, there were lots of smaller chains and local rental shops, but no one could touch Blockbuster's brand awareness, customer base, or retail footprint. They owned the video rental market— until they didn't. Fast Company interviewed Blockbuster CEO Jim Keyes and asked, "Do you ever see a way that Netflix could overtake Blockbuster as the global market leader?" Keyes replied, "I don't—we have such different business models. There is a wonderful role for the Netflix service in the marketplace, but it's very different from ours. I think we coexist quite well with Netflix."[1]

It took Blockbuster six years after Netflix launched just to realize they needed to enter the video rental-by-mail space. At which time, the CEO said: "I've been frankly confused by this fascination that everybody has with Netflix . . . Netflix doesn't really have or do anything that we can't or don't already do ourselves." As TechCrunch so poignantly said, "Blockbuster was already dead—they just didn't realize it yet."[2]

Could Blockbuster have held its Unrivaled market position? Yes. Were they open and willing to Adapt to changing market forces to keep their place as number one? No.

Complacency is a business killer. There is no set it and forget it when you are Unrivaled. Unrivaled brands have incredible staying power, but nothing lasts forever. Savvy leaders know that the only constant in business is change. Even after you achieve Unrivaled status, you can't take your eye off the ball. As a VC once told me, "You're only on top until a competitor emerges to eat your lunch."

You've worked hard to be Unrivaled. That's why the final step in the Unrivaled Growth Framework is to *stay* Unrivaled.

CHAPTER 32

PROTECTING YOUR UNRIVALED MOAT

As we noted in an earlier chapter, the legendary investor Warren Buffett describes the best companies as having a "moat" around their castle. That's how I think of Unrivaled companies. They have a moat that protects them from attack, secures their leadership position, and gives them staying power. It also gives you a new way of looking at growth.

Instead of worrying about people storming the castle, once you have a moat around your castle, you can play a different kind of game. Because you have taken the steps to create distance from your competitors, it's harder for them to touch you. You've created separation. That doesn't mean you're cut off from your market or hunkered down inside your castle. It just means you are well-defended. Instead of being reactive, you can be proactive. You're looking out, ahead, and around the corner. You are free to play offense. You can take risks, build, grow, invest, and expand—you are in step with your ideal customer without constantly trying to copy what the competition is doing.

But even moats can dry up if left unattended. You have built a moat with your Unrivaled Growth Framework. Now you need to keep it wide and deep.

For starters, the more successful you are, the more competition you will attract. New players and old rivals will march on your castle, and your moat needs to stay strong in order to withstand the four biggest threats to Unrivaled status:

1. A nimble new competitor.
   - Solution: Adapt to preserve your Ownable Whitespace.

2. A change in your customers' reality.
   - Solution: Stay obsessed with your customers.

3. Complacency.
   - Solution: Evolve and innovate your go-to-market.

4. External or unpredictable crises.
   - Solution: Use your Business Ethos to turn headwinds into tailwinds.

Let's take a look at how some of the most successful companies adapted to stay Unrivaled and how their success can inform your ability to stay Unrivaled.

Protect Your Moat
Stay Unrivaled!

Moat Protector #1: Stay Ahead of New Competitors by Preserving Your Ownable Whitespace (Or: *Let the Force Be with You*)

Salesforce is one of the world's leading Customer Relationship Management (CRM) platforms. Founded in 1999, Salesforce introduced a cloud-based, subscription-based model that disrupted the CRM industry, moving away from traditional on-premises solutions. This approach allowed businesses of all sizes to access powerful CRM capabilities without the need for significant upfront investment in hardware or infrastructure. By carving out this Ownable Whitespace and offering a unique benefit to its ideal customers, Salesforce quickly became the Unrivaled leader in their field.

Their success, however, attracted a slew of competitors, all jumping into the pool to offer competing cloud-based solutions that threatened to eat away at Salesforce's market share. Meanwhile, the digital revolution presented nonstop change for all SaaS companies, further threatening to breach Salesforce's moat.

So how did Salesforce remain Unrivaled? By continuing to Commit to—and evolve—their Ownable Whitespace. Salesforce knew it would not be the CRM solution for *every* business, but they committed to maintaining market leadership for the specific target market they served. Thus, they protected their Ownable Whitespace as the top choice for large, enterprise businesses by keeping a strong focus on product innovation as well as regularly introducing new features, enhancements, and integrations to its CRM platform specifically tailored to their ideal customer bullseye. This commitment to innovation has helped Salesforce stay ahead of the curve and meet the evolving needs of its ideal customers in areas such as sales, marketing, customer service, and analytics.

Over the years, Salesforce has also expanded its product portfolio beyond CRM to offer a comprehensive suite of cloud-based business applications and enterprise solutions. This includes acquisitions and developments in areas such as e-commerce (Commerce Cloud), collaboration (Salesforce Chatter), and analytics (Tableau). Salesforce has pursued strategic acquisitions and partnerships to complement its core offerings and expand its market reach.[1] All of these changes have been driven by what their ideal customer's highest needs were.

Salesforce understands that meeting their customer's needs and desires, even as those demands change and the competitive landscape evolves, is the key to preserving their Ownable Whitespace and staying Unrivaled.

Speaking of customers, that brings us to moat protector #2 . . .

Moat Protector #2: As Your Customer's Reality Evolves, Stay Obsessed (Or: *Sometimes It's Okay to Be a Hog*)

Harley-Davidson® motorcycles are perfectly geared to their ideal customer bullseye. Harleys are big, loud, and fast. They are made for riders who seek the "open road." Even people who have never owned or driven one of their motorcycles have a strong impression of the Harley-Davidson brand.

Childhood friends William Harley and Arthur Davidson established the company in Milwaukee, Wisconsin, in 1903. By 1920, they had dealers in over sixty-seven countries and were the largest motorcycle manufacturer in the world. During WWII, the company played a major role supporting the US military, producing ninety thousand motorcycles during the war.

But no company is guaranteed Unrivaled status forever. In 1969, the company was sold and restructured. Employees were cut. Harley-Davidson struggled to keep up with foreign competition, leading to lower-quality products and unhappy customers. Bankruptcy loomed.

The company was sold again in 1981, this time to a management group that included William Davidson of the original Davidson family owners. The new ownership realized they had to make a dramatic shift—not just to regain Unrivaled status but to survive.

Instead of moving toward the newer foreign bike standards—lighter, agile, cheaper—and doing what other motorcycle companies were doing, Harley doubled down on its ideal customer bullseye. Who were the customers who were Harley-obsessed? What did they like? What did they want? What made them choose Harley? Harley-Davidson refocused on what their ideal customer wanted—big, loud, traditional models. Harley rededicated their product focus to the standard big bike approach, epitomized by the new "Fat Boy" model. They leaned into their bullseye, adding branded products, clubs, and even restaurants, all built on the Harley brand. They even changed their stock ticker to HOG—standing for Harley Owners Group and serving as a continual throwback to the baby pig from one of the most famous Harley-Davidson photos.

Harley understood that great brands never lose sight of their ideal customer bullseye. More than one hundred years after they started riding Harleys, fans still know they can count on their HOG.

Variety Is the Spice of Life

Unrivaled companies know that everything starts with the customer. But how do you stay Unrivaled when the demands of growth—or the realities of demographics—force you to set your sights on a new ideal customer?

That was the dilemma facing Old Spice, and their solution is a perfect case study in how to Adapt and *stay* Unrivaled.

When Procter & Gamble bought Old Spice in 1990 for $300 million, the company was a leading brand in men's shaving and aftershave. It had a loyal customer base built over fifty years. My grandfather was one of those loyal customers. He used his Old Spice aftershave every day and said it made him "look younger." But the reality for Old Spice was that most of their customers were my grandfather's age and getting older. In fact, no one under forty wanted anything to do with this product line that was geared toward an older generation of men. Procter & Gamble realized they had to dramatically shift their focus to appeal to a younger audience before it was too late.

So Old Spice pointed their arrow at a new target market: eighteen-to-thirty-five-year-olds. And they *obsessed* about this new ideal customer. They appealed to this younger audience through humor and personality. They developed campaigns that poked fun at dated concepts of manliness and the unattainable expectations of the real world. From their ad campaigns to website content and social media, the Old Spice brand adopted a new voice and attitude that was completely curated for this younger audience.

They also discovered that 50 percent of bodywash purchases were made by women, so Old Spice created an ad campaign to appeal to this decision-maker as well. The "Man Your Man Can Smell Like" commercial featured the (impressively hunky) actor Isaiah Mustafa and promised women that even if their man wasn't Mustafa, he could still smell like him.

The campaigns went viral. Old Spice enjoyed forty million YouTube views after just one week, and their Twitter followers increased by 2,700 percent. Traffic to oldspice.com doubled.

Sales results were just as astounding, increasing 125 percent in just one year. Old Spice became the number one brand for men's bodywash.[2]

Perhaps the most fascinating element of all was that Old Spice didn't change its product line at all. Instead, it adapted its message to appeal to a new target market and stayed Unrivaled.

Moat Protector #3: Evolve and Innovate to Give Your Ideal Customers What They Want Even Before They Know (Or: *What's the Ending to This Movie?*)

We talked about how Netflix displaced Blockbuster by offering DVD rentals by mail. Netflix offered an innovative solution, while Blockbuster was doomed by complacency. But that was just the first chapter in the Netflix story.

By 2005, Netflix was shipping more than one million DVDs in the US every day. It would have been easy for cofounder and chairman Reed Hastings to sit back and enjoy the company's Unrivaled spot as king of the DVD rental world. But he knew that his company's Vision was not to provide cheaper and more convenient DVD rentals—it was to reduce friction in accessing entertainment. And access was about to undergo a revolutionary change.

So Netflix turned their attention to streaming, and in 2007 they launched their online streaming service, "Watch Now." It's almost hard to remember, but back in 2007, streaming was neither simple nor widespread. Yet Netflix knew that its customers were constantly seeking more convenient and immediate ways to watch videos, and streaming was the future. So Netflix invested $40 million in streaming technology and put themselves years ahead of their competitors. They built a user-friendly interface powered by a robust engine providing personalized recommendations and trailers. By the time other distribution companies (think cable TV, network TV, and movie theaters) jumped onto the streaming bandwagon, Netflix had a big head start.

When the pandemic struck in 2020, keeping everyone home and searching for entertainment, Netflix was in the power position, and its streaming business exploded.

But Netflix still wasn't done innovating. By 2022, streaming growth had cooled off and dozens of competitors had jumped in the pool, including Disney, Amazon Prime, HBO, Hulu, Peacock, and more. Netflix lost customers in early 2022 and had to lay off hundreds of employees. So they evolved yet again by doubling down on original content.

Netflix had laid the groundwork for this next adaptation too. Back in 2013, Netflix stunned their competitors by producing and airing a blockbuster series, *House of Cards*. The show featured A-list stars, award-winning production quality, and a storyline that captured the entire country's imagination. From that point on, Netflix invested heavily in high-quality original content, which enabled them to weather the storms of streaming service demand.

Netflix has consistently evolved to delight, engage, and expand their customer base. Even when they cracked down on password sharing, they added an ad-based model to provide a lower-cost subscription option. They also expanded worldwide, not just in subscribers but in production hubs around the globe, which meant lower-cost options for producing content. They've recently added more reality TV content, more live TV, and more sports content (including super popular sports documentaries). Meanwhile, other entertainment companies are increasingly licensing their content to Netflix, realizing that it's better to access Netflix's subscribers than compete head-on. In other words, if you can't beat 'em, join 'em.

Netflix is a textbook case of evolving to innovate offerings, growing to meet customers' demands, leveraging new technology, and staying ahead of the competition while always being driven by their Vision: "to entertain the world." Because they Obsess about their ideal customers, they are able to continue to offer what matters to them most and they continue to Differentiate themselves as the number one choice for lovers of excellent streaming content.

The results speak for themselves: Netflix is the top subscription streaming company in the world, with 260 million paying customers and a net income of $33.7 billion.[3]

Moat Protector #4: Turn Headwinds into Tailwinds (Or: *It's Not Your Fault, but It Is Your Problem*)

One of the toughest things any CEO has to deal with is an unexpected crisis. The dot-com bust, 9/11, the banking collapse, a worldwide pandemic, a product recall, a corporate scandal. Disasters come to even the best-run businesses, and how you weather the storm will determine your future.

For example, the COVID pandemic was devastating for many families and many businesses; it also changed the landscape of how consumers make buying decisions. In that transformed landscape, new brands were crowned and old brands were deposed from their Unrivaled status.

The temptation in a crisis is bottom-line thinking—we'll just hunker down and throttle back! You start thinking it's cheaper to cut marketing, customer service, loyalty programs, or all of the above. Do more with less and focus everything and everyone on efficiency. But here's the rub— you're making everything less efficient. You end up being penny-wise and pound-foolish. The best protection against crisis is to lean into your Unrivaled Growth Framework. Focus even harder on your ideal customer bullseye. Prioritize messaging and channels that create Surround Sound, spotlight your Ownable Whitespace, and reinforce your Business Ethos.

One of the worst tampering scandals in history is also one of the best examples of how a brand handled a crisis. In 1982, seven people died suddenly after taking TYLENOL® that had been laced with cyanide. The media coverage was swift and overwhelming as well as potentially devastating to a brand that was the most successful over-the-counter product in the country. At the time, more than a hundred million people used TYLENOL for minor aches and pains. Suddenly, it was at the center of a deadly poisoning spree.

Parent company Johnson & Johnson did exactly what an Unrivaled company does: they put the welfare of their customers first. According to many studies of the case, the J&J chairman immediately formed a seven-person task force and gave the following instructions: First, "How do we protect the people?" Second, "How do we save this product?"[4] J&J recalled millions of bottles of TYLENOL off the shelves—first in Chicago and soon thereafter across the entire country. They aired TV and radio commercials everywhere, warning people not to consume TYLENOL. The company established a 1-800 hotline for consumers to call. They also established a toll-free line for news organizations to call and receive prerecorded daily messages with updated statements about the crisis.

Johnson & Johnson used earned media as well—they held several major press conferences at company headquarters, and the chairman did in-depth interviews on *60 Minutes* and other national shows within days of the crisis.

In addition, Johnson & Johnson immediately embarked on redesigning their packaging for greater security; they basically invented tamperproof packaging, with all other over-the-counter products eventually following their lead.

In 1982, TYLENOL had 37 percent of the painkiller market, outselling its next four competitors combined. At the time of the crisis, TYLENOL was responsible for 19 percent of the profits of the entire company. Recalling the product and spending millions on ads warning customers not to use it could have been devastating to their brand.

Instead, Johnson & Johnson's quick and deliberate action positioned them as the victim of a terrible crime and as champions of their customers' safety. In less than five months, TYLENOL had relaunched and fully regained its market share.[5]

Staying Unrivaled requires that you regularly check in to be sure your strategy is in tune with your target market and your competitive landscape. Markets change, customers evolve, and competitors are constantly coming up with new ways to steal away your customers and supplant you as their number one choice.

You have to be willing to Adapt if you want to remain Unrivaled.

CHAPTER 33

CHANGES ON THE HORIZON: STAYING UNRIVALED THROUGH MERGERS, ACQUISITIONS, AND AI

One of the biggest changes for Unrivaled companies comes when they enter a new stage of growth. You work twenty-four-seven to reach Unrivaled, and the payoff is that you're so successful you can actually acquire one (or more) of your rivals, vendors, or partners. Good news.

Until this shoe drops: you now have two, three, or four brands to manage—not just one. If you try to juggle them all, you can wind up driving a brand clown car. Too many brands are squeezed into one space, all fighting for attention. The same thing happens when private equity firms buy up companies and try to put them all together into one brand. Some are executed well. Others are a mess of brand confusion in the marketplace. The brand clown car is expensive and inefficient, and it creates confusion for the customers who just came along for the acquisition or merger ride.

What do you do when you have four companies that were all doing their own go-to-markets, with their own target markets, with their own *everything*, now trying to come together as one new entity and one new brand? How do you bring four brands together as one? Are these all the same ideal customers, wanting the same thing, pursuing the same Mission, prioritizing the same benefits? Or should you keep several distinct brands?

Are you going to have a branded house or a house of brands?

At Growth Street, we've worked with many of our clients through mergers and acquisitions. One of our clients, a Fortune 500 life sciences company, acquires ten to fifteen companies a year. That's a lot of brands to care for, feed, and keep growing. My advice to them has remained the same throughout: lean into the powerful household brand you have built and fold the smaller brands into that one Unrivaled brand.

There's no doubt that sometimes it does make sense for an acquiring company to keep multiple brands, although my caution is always the same: it can be an expensive proposition in terms of time, resources, and money. In some cases, like for Marriott brands, it makes total sense—The Ritz-Carlton® is different from the SpringHill Suites. Their ideal customers are different and the go-to-market is different, so it wouldn't make sense to fold them all together unless they decided to double down on a specific ideal customer. On the other hand, for our life sciences client, continuing that Unrivaled status by investing in one brand is the force multiplier. Either way, decide and avoid brand confusion and inefficiency.

Acquired Customers Are Gold

The biggest threat to your Unrivaled status during mergers and acquisitions is losing sight of your customers. You have just paid millions—maybe billions—to acquire a company, and one of the key assets you bought was their customer base. When I worked for J.P. Morgan, E*TRADE Financial acquired the business I was helping to run, BrownCo. The average account balance of a BrownCo customer was the highest in the industry at around $160,000. With over two hundred thousand accounts and multimillion-dollar margin balances, you can quickly do the math on why E*TRADE wanted to keep every single one of those accounts!

The biggest question BrownCo customers had when the acquisition was announced was: "What's going to happen to me?" As I probed deeper into their specific fears and concerns, other questions came to the surface: "Is the price going to change? Is my account rep the same person or someone new? Do I have to move to a new platform? What happens to all of my historical data?"

Just remember: your newly acquired customers might not be quite as excited about this transaction as you are. While the merging companies are doing high fives, the customer is often lost in the shuffle, worrying about an uncertain future. As the business leader, you are often in "spreadsheet mode," concerned with deal ROI, reducing redundancy, integrating operations, and all the other ways to maximize efficiencies. Instead of just focusing on the transaction, channel your customer obsession and think about your new customers as gold. Don't just start trying to cross-sell them products and services. Maximize the full value! Make sure someone on your team is tasked with:

- Understanding what your newly acquired customers care about— what are their favorite things about the company you just bought, and what are they worried about with this transition? How are these new customers different from your existing customers? Are they the same ideal customer persona?

- Creating a communication plan for your new customers—and your existing ones—to explain the journey that lies ahead.

- Explaining to your new customers how they will be successful with you. (You might not be able to keep everything they liked about their old provider, but you do have plenty to offer them, so be sure you share that with them.)

- Whether you're merging or acquiring, preserving and transferring customer loyalty is the surest way to navigate a merger or acquisition, achieve deal ROI, and stay Unrivaled.

Unrivaled in the Age of AI

Let's look at one more threat to Unrivaled companies—a change of historic significance.

In the late eighteenth century, the Industrial Revolution spelled opportunity—and disaster—for countless businesses and dozens of industries. Two hundred years later, the digital revolution had a similar game-changing effect. Today, we are witnessing yet another revolution that is fundamentally changing the way work gets done: the artificial intelligence (AI) revolution.

Of course, a form of AI has been at our fingertips for years, powering everything from searches to chatbots. Lots of technology start-ups were built on AI, and it forged new market opportunities to disrupt age-old ways of doing things across health care, construction, financial services, advertising, and others—no industry is untouched.

As I'm writing this sentence, multiple new AI products and applications are launching on the scene every day. Virtually every business is experimenting with AI in some fashion, and most businesses see immediate opportunities to use AI to create content, to ingest and analyze gigantic volumes of data, and to automate customer service processes. No doubt the time and cost savings will be enormous—but, at least for now, AI still needs human involvement if you want to stay Unrivaled.

As you use AI to create social media or web content, for example, or to diagnose trends or better triage your customer service inquiries and resolution, make sure you preserve the authenticity of your brand. AI *might* be able to mimic your brand voice, it *might* correctly communicate your Core Values, or it *might* diagnose a specific customer complaint. But it will not be able to do so without guidance.

Good AI requires "training"—you must invest the time to "teach" AI your voice and all the elements of your Brand Manifesto. Otherwise, your new content will sound like a computer wrote it. Good AI also requires human oversight. AI might do 90 percent of the work, but that last 10 percent—the review and quality control that requires human judgment—might just be the difference between customer satisfaction and customer alienation.

Remember: your most valuable asset is the trust and loyalty of your customers. It's hard for a machine to create trust. So, as AI becomes ubiquitous, evolve wisely and experiment carefully.

KEY LEARNINGS
FOR STEP 5
ADAPT

There are no guarantees in business. Even Unrivaled companies come under attack or fall from grace. That's why the final step in our Unrivaled Growth Framework shows you how to stay Unrivaled and turn headwinds into tailwinds. The key, as we've seen, is to Adapt. Specifically, that means:

1. Keep your eye on the competition, but don't copy them!

2. Stay in lockstep with the ever-changing needs of your ideal customer bullseye of today and tomorrow.

3. Look for ways to innovate and evolve to maintain your Ownable Whitespace.

4. Be proactive in a crisis and lean into your Business Ethos.

5. Don't lose sight of your brand when you grow, especially when it comes to mergers and acquisitions.

6. Prioritize authenticity as you use AI in your business.

CONCLUSION
TIME TO GIDDY UP!

"Embrace what you don't know, especially in the beginning, because what you don't know can become your greatest asset. It ensures that you will absolutely be doing things different from everybody else."

—SARA BLAKELY, FOUNDER AND CEO, SPANX®

Congratulations! You have achieved Unrivaled status! As a CEO who went through one of my Unrivaled growth workshops emphatically said, "We are Unrivalers!" Hearing someone internalize the power of being Unrivaled gave me goose bumps! And now, you are an Unrivaler too. You've done the hard work to figure out your North Star Vision, Mission, and Core Values. You've obsessed about your ideal customers. You've found your Ownable Whitespace and captured it in your Unique Value Proposition (UVP). You've put it all together in your Brand Manifesto, and your entire team is aligned and committed. Your go-to-market execution is optimized and in perfect Surround Sound. And you know how to Adapt and stay Unrivaled when market dynamics change or headwinds start blowing. ***Giddy Up!***

Unrivaled = Explosive Business Growth

Throughout this book, together we have learned the benefits of becoming Unrivaled—streamlining efficiency, eliminating friction, maximizing your marketing efforts, engaging and inspiring your team, and building unbreakable trust and loyalty with your customers.

The ultimate benefit of Unrivaled is, of course, explosive business growth. As an Unrivaled company, your business is not just successful—it is unstoppable. You blow past benchmarks and race over speed bumps that sideline or stagnate your competitors. You play offense, not defense. You're in a league of your own.

The Unrivaled Growth Framework delivers a proven road map to help you reach and exceed your business goals, to get you unstuck from stalled growth, shrinking margins, stiff economic headwinds, or just the normal friction of hot competition in a fast-changing business landscape. The road map creates a moat around your brand that ensures exceptional profits and unstoppable growth.

As we've outlined in the preceding chapters, first you need to be obsessed with your ideal customers, who they are, and how they make decisions. Then you must put a stake in the ground: *this* is what we stand for, *this* is why we exist, this is our Business Ethos. Through strategic differentiation from your competitors, you carve out your Ownable Whitespace, the place where you are best at providing what your ideal customer wants and needs the most. This Ownable Whitespace can be boiled down into one short and sweet statement: your UVP.

What you stand for (your Business Ethos) and how you stand apart (your Ownable Whitespace) will drive your Visual Identity—the visual and external representation of who you are, why you exist, and how you help your ideal customer. This Visual Identity will help you stand out, and by putting it all into your Brand Manifesto, you have the playbook for your entire team. You get everyone aligned with your brand and Commit to using it as a guide for every business decision you make.

We've also reviewed the winding path of your ideal customer's buyer's journey and how their purchase decision affects your go-to-market. By matching all of your go-to-market strategies with your ideal customer's buyer's journey, you create Surround Sound, Execute efficiently, cut the waste, and maximize the ROI on every part of your go-to-market.

Unrivaled companies achieve explosive yet sustainable business growth and extraordinary Customer Lifetime Value (CLV) without the friction and frustration of most other companies. By following our Unrivaled Growth

Framework, you have the clarity that makes all future business decisions simpler. You avoid wasted time, wasted energy, and wasted money, all by following the road map you've built. When new competitors nip at your heels or new technology threatens your Ownable Whitespace, you have the tools you need to confidently Adapt and stay ahead of the curve. You are set up for long-term success.

Fighting for market share is grueling. Keeping up the pace of early growth while protecting and improving margins is tougher than ever. Incorporating new technology and navigating change while maintaining ROI is daunting.

Give yourself the market leader advantage.

Embrace our five-step growth framework.

Be Unrivaled.

Being Unrivaled

Perhaps one of the best examples of being Unrivaled is captured in the story of Nike. (It's such a great story, they made a movie about it! If you haven't seen it, *Air* stars two of my favorite Bostonians, Ben Affleck and Matt Damon, and is a powerful lesson in strategic brand differentiation.)

Nike is Unrivaled.

But it wasn't always that way.

In the early '80s, sales were stagnating, and Nike struggled to grow. They lacked brand awareness, and their competitors, like adidas and Converse, were leading the market and eating their lunch. They needed a bold move to shake things up, leapfrog the competition, and stand out.

Sonny Vaccaro had the answer. As a company executive, he knew Nike had to do something big and bold to stand out and grow. He remembered seeing a player a few years earlier named Michael Jordan. He remembered Jordan's unique moves and charismatic personality and thought he would be perfect for Nike.

The problem was Jordan didn't know Nike. He had never heard of the brand.

That was when Vaccaro remembered one of Nike's Core Values: "We're on offense. All the time." Empowered and committed, Vaccaro convinced

Nike to go all in on Jordan. Then he walked the talk. He showed Jordan that they were more than a shoe company and even built a relationship with Jordan's mom. Vaccaro helped Jordan take the Nike brand seriously. The rest is "Just Do It" history.[1]

To this day, the internal memo that created the foundation for Nike's brand provides compelling inspiration. They use their Business Ethos to Differentiate. They Commit and Execute flawlessly. They Adapt with their customers and leave their competitors in the dust.

1. Our business is change.

2. We're on offense. All the time.

3. Perfect results count -- not a perfect process.
   Break the rules: fight the law.

4. This is as much about battle as about business.

5. Assume nothing.
   Make sure people keep their promises.
   Push yourselves push others.
   Stretch the possible.

6. Live off the land.

7. Your job isn't done until the job is done.

8. Dangers
   Bureaucracy
   Personal ambition
   Energy takers vs. energy givers
   Knowing our weaknesses
   Don't get too many things on the platter

9. It won't be pretty.

10. If we do the right things we'll make money damn
    near automatic.

2

Nike boasts annual worldwide sales of over $30 billion—they also boast incredible brand loyalty, with one hundred million members of their customer loyalty program spending three times as much as other shoppers. Along the way, Nike has kept its finger firmly on the pulse of its ideal customer, ensuring that every element of its go-to-market is aligned—from the swoosh logo, to its celebrity influencers, to the design of the stores, to the brilliant use of their app to guide the buyer's journey, to the explosion of their direct-to-consumer channel.

Today, Nike doesn't even need to put their name on their products—just the iconic swoosh or the Jordan leap logo is enough to say to consumers what Nike says consistently across all its messaging: we get you. Nike's Mission: to bring inspiration and innovation to every athlete in the world. And as Nike puts it, "If you have a body, you are an athlete." They are customer obsessed.

Yet Nike is not afraid to offend, not afraid to take a stand. Again, they know their ideal customer so well, they can lean into headlines and trends without appearing fake or losing trust. It's a powerful position built on years of creating a powerful moat around their Ownable Whitespace and never straying from their Business Ethos. Nike's universal commitment to their target market and their Mission has helped Nike become—and stay—Unrivaled.[3]

Oh, and before you go . . .

Pay It Forward

I was waiting in the Starbucks drive-through. The line was snaking around the building, and we had been sitting for what seemed like an eternity. Finally, the line started moving. As I went to move forward, the person in the car behind me laid on the horn and yelled out his window at me, "Let's go, lady!" Annoyed and stunned, I inched forward to the window to get my order. The associate was clearly frazzled, and the guy behind me beeping his horn certainly didn't help. I said, "I'd like to pay for the person behind me." The associate was shocked. "Really? Why do you want to pay for them when they were so rude and they keep beeping at you?" The reality is that we don't always know what someone else is going through. Maybe his boss is a jerk and makes his life miserable when he's late. Maybe he got in a fight with his spouse and is having a bad day. Maybe his business is failing and he doesn't know what to do.

In my work with my clients, I spend a lot of time considering alternate perspectives—putting myself in someone else's shoes. These insights give me context and create new learnings and information, both for me and for my clients.

As you now go forward to whatever your day brings, I encourage you to pay your new Unrivaled knowledge forward. Who could benefit from knowing what you now know? What can you accomplish together at your company with a new common understanding? How could you help someone solve a problem by thinking differently about the solution? Knowledge is the gift that keeps on giving. Who will you share *Unrivaled* with today?

Giddy Up!

Bonus Materials

As you apply the strategies and concepts in the Five-Step Unrivaled Growth Framework, go to michelleheath.com to access additional *Unrivaled* materials. Please don't hesitate to reach out—I'd love to hear from you. **Giddy Up!**

ENDNOTES

CHAPTER 1

1. "Ethos." Wikipedia, April 20, 2024. https://en.wikipedia.org/wiki/Ethos.
2. Chandler, Robert. "Wells Fargo, American Corporation." Encyclopædia Britannica, 2024. https://www.britannica.com/money/Wells-Fargo-American-corporation.
3. History of Wells Fargo, 2024. https://www.wellsfargo.com/about/corporate/history/.
4. "Wells Fargo—a Timeline of Recent Consumer Protection and Corporate Governance Scandals." Congressional Research Service, 2020. https://crsreports.congress.gov/product/pdf/IF/IF11129.
5. Ibid.
6. "Leadership and Governance." Leadership and Governance—Wells Fargo. Accessed May 15, 2024. https://www.wellsfargo.com/about/corporate/governance/#codeofethics.
7. "The Value of Keeping the Right Customers." *Harvard Business Review*, November 5, 2014. https://hbr.org/2014/10/the-value-of-keeping-the-right-customers.
8. Kim, Tae. "Warren Buffett Believes This Is 'the Most Important Thing' to Find in a Business." CNBC, May 7, 2018. https://www.cnbc.com/2018/05/07/warren-buffett-believes-this-is-the-most-important-thing-to-find-in-a-business.html.
9. "Morning Session—1995 Berkshire Hathaway Meeting." CNBC, November 28, 2018. https://buffett.cnbc.com/video/1995/05/01/morning-session---1995-berkshire-hathaway-annual-meeting.html?&start=6671&end=7022.
10. Romero, Jessie. "The Rise and Fall of Circuit City," Economic History, 2013. https://www.richmondfed.org/~/media/richmondfedorg/publications/research/econ_focus/2013/q3/pdf/economic_history.pdf.
11. "Why a Tornado Prompted Best Buy to Change Its Original Name." CBC News, March 10, 2022. https://www.cbc.ca/radio/undertheinfluence/why-a-tornado-prompted-best-buy-to-change-its-original-name-1.6371296.

12. Buday, Catherine, and Jon Eckhardt. "Timeless Lessons from Dick Schulze." *Entrepreneur & Innovation Exchange*, December 29, 2020. https://eiexchange.com/content/timeless-lessons-from-dick-schulze.

13. Romero, Jessie. "The Rise and Fall of Circuit City," *Econ Focus* Vol. 17, Iss. 3 (2013): https://www.richmondfed.org/~/media/richmondfedorg/publications/research/econ_focus/2013/q3/pdf/economic_history.pdf.

CHAPTER 3

1. "About Kizuna." The Government of Japan. Accessed May 15, 2024. https://www.japan.go.jp/kizuna/about_kizuna.html.

2. "2020 U.S. Automotive Brand Loyalty Study | J.D. Power." J.D. Power. Accessed May 16, 2024. https://www.jdpower.com/business/press-releases/2020-us-automotive-brand-loyalty-study.

3. Squiz. "Marketing and Content Teams: A Step-by-Step Guide to Web Personalization [with Templates]." Squiz, July 20, 2023. https://www.squiz.net/blog/step-by-step-guide-to-web-personalization.
Ozzy Osbourne: F darkbladeus, Ozzy Osbourne, Prince of Darkness, at the I Am Ozzy book signing at Changing Hands, Tempe Arizona, Feb 20th, 2010. Public domain photograph via Wikimedia Commons.
King Charles: Created by modifying "Official portrait of Charles, Prince of Wales in New Zealand, 2019" (© Mark Tantrum (Licensed under CC BY 4.0)). https://creativecommons.org/licenses/by/4.0/.

4. "Subaru Barrels Through Recession." NBCNews.com, May 31, 2010. https://www.nbcnews.com/id/wbna37274797.

5. Ibid.

6. Holmes, Jake. "How 'Love' Helped Kick-Start Subaru Sales in the U.S." Motor1, April 17, 2017. https://www.motor1.com/news/142732/subaru-love-ad-campaign/.

7. "Forbes Recognizes Subaru as One of America's Best Brands for Social Impact—Subaru U.S. Media Center." https://media.subaru.com, April 26, 2023. https://media.subaru.com/newsrelease.do?id=2044.

8. "Subaru Highest Ranked Mainstream Suvs in 2023 J.D. Power Customer Loyalty Rankings." https://media.subaru.com, November 21, 2023. https://media.subaru.com/pressrelease/2125/1/subaru-highest-ranked-mainstream-suvs-2023-j.d-power#:~:text=Subaru%20of%20America%2C%20Inc.

CHAPTER 5

1. "Alan Cooper." Wikipedia, April 29, 2024. https://en.wikipedia.org/wiki/Alan_Cooper.

CHAPTER 7

1. Bajaj, Vikas. "E*Trade to Buy BrownCo from J.P. Morgan for $1.6 Billion." *New York Times*, September 29, 2005. https://www.nytimes.com/2005/09/29/business/etrade-to-buy-brownco-from-jp-morgan-for-16-billion.html.

CHAPTER 9

1. "The Role Core Values Play in Strategy Execution: HBS Online." Business Insights Blog, November 21, 2023. https://online.hbs.edu/blog/post/how-to-implement-core-values-in-the-workplace.

CHAPTER 12

1. "The Role Core Values Play in Strategy Execution: HBS Online." Business Insights Blog, November 21, 2023. https://online.hbs.edu/blog/post/how-to-implement-core-values-in-the-workplace?c1=GAW_CM_NW&source=US_GEN_PMAX&cr2=content__-__us__-__gen__-__pmax&kw=general&cr5=&cr6=&cr7=c&utm_campaign=content__-__us__-__gen__-__pmax&utm_term=general&gad_source=1&gclid=CjwKCAiAiP2tBhBXEiwACslfnp3dUFUYIWyr9kawAg38KxGZgyFbl_p_HpyfwYkuEi2LPstt76vN9hoClZQQAvD_BwE.

CHAPTER 13

1. Pendell, Ryan. "Customer Brand Preference and Decisions: Gallup's 70/30 Principle." Gallup.com, March 8, 2024. https://www.gallup.com/workplace/398954/customer-brand-preference-decisions-gallup-principle.aspx.
2. Langford, Robin. "Emotional Engagement with Consumers 'Could Boost Retail Sales 5%.'" Netimperative, December 6, 2017. https://www.netimperative.com/2017/12/06/emotional-engagement-consumers-boost-retail-sales-5/.
3. Ibid.
4. "Business Unusual." Patagonia. Accessed May 15, 2024. https://www.patagonia.com/business-unusual/.
5. Patagonia. March 10, 2023. Patagonia on LinkedIn. https://www.linkedin.com/posts/patagonia_2_patagonia50th-activity-7040002514741600256--G_n?utm_source=share&utm_medium=member_desktop.

CHAPTER 14

1. Bishop, Lucy. "What Influences an Hermès Birkin Bag Price." Sotheby's, April 8, 2024. https://www.sothebys.com/en/articles/what-influences-an-hermes-birkin-bag-price.
2. Ibid.

CHAPTER 15

1. Reynolds, Siimon. *When They Zig, You Zag*. Limited Edition, Pan Macmillan Australia Pty, 1998.

CHAPTER 16

1. "History." Warby Parker. Accessed May 15, 2024. https://www.warbyparker.com/history.
2. Rius, Anton. "How to Create a Unique Value Proposition in a Crowded Market." Corporate Visions, December 13, 2022. https://corporatevisions.com/unique-value-proposition/.

CHAPTER 17

1. Note: This is not Subaru-approved positioning. It is using Subaru as an example of what the framework could look like. "More than a Car Company—Subaru." Our Drive for Impact 2022 Subaru of America Corporate Impact Report, June 21, 2023. https://ourimpact.subaru.com/more-than-a-car-company/.

CHAPTER 18

1. Admin. "What Airbnb Teaches Us About Having a Strong Brand Identity." SOCi, December 19, 2023. https://www.meetsoci.com/resources/blog/localized-marketing/.what-airbnb-teaches-us-about-having-a-strong-brand-identity/
2. Symonds, Cat, and Jose. "The Rule of 7: The Power of Social Media." Factorial, January 16, 2024. https://factorialhr.com/blog/the-rule-of-7/.

CHAPTER 19

1. Howarth, Josh. "81 Online Review Statistics (New 2024 Data)." Exploding Topics, December 1, 2023. https://explodingtopics.com/blog/online-review-stats
2. "Our People—Subaru." Our Drive for Impact 2022 Subaru of America Corporate Impact Report, July 17, 2023. https://ourimpact.subaru.com/our-people/.
3. "Our People—Subaru." Our Drive for Impact 2022 Subaru of America Corporate Impact Report, July 17, 2023. https://ourimpact.subaru.com/our-people/.

CHAPTER 22

1. SuperOffice. "Key Customer Experience Statistics to Know." 32 Customer Experience Statistics for 2024, May 4, 2024. https://www.superoffice.com/blog/customer-experience-statistics.

2. "Nike: B2B Marketing Lessons from Lauren Fleshman's Visionary 'Objectify Me' Campaign with Kaite Rosa, Senior Director of Brand at Axonius." Spotify. Accessed May 15, 2024. https://open.spotify.com/episode/1tr8Y2oHFrqUd 8S8EAdw58?si=KrYYTYNCSlmYwYm8qgd6Cw&nd=1.

CHAPTER 23

1. "Better Grower Program." Divine Flavor, November 24, 2023. https://divineflavor.com/index.php/better-grower-program/.

CHAPTER 24

1. "The B2B Buying Journey: Key Stages and How to Optimize Them." Gartner. Accessed May 16, 2024. https://www.gartner.com/en/sales/insights/b2b-buying-journey.
2. Smith, Jacqueline. "What Is Dark Social?" Hallam, May 15, 2023. https://www.hallaminternet.com/what-is-dark-social/.
3. Kowalewicz, Rebecca. "Council Post: Understanding and Utilizing Dark Social in Marketing." *Forbes*, August 21, 2023. https://www.forbes.com/sites/forbesagencycouncil/2023/08/18/understanding-and-utilizing-dark-social-in-marketing/?sh=37e264655449.

CHAPTER 25

1. "What B2Bs Need to Know About Their Buyers." *Harvard Business Review*, September 22, 2022. https://hbr.org/2022/09/what-b2bs-need-to-know-about-their-buyers.

CHAPTER 26

1. Pymnts. "Influencers Help Brands Drive Sales Through Retail Media Networks." PYMNTS.com, May 11, 2023. https://www.pymnts.com/news/retail/2023/influencers-help-brands-drive-sales-through-retail-media-networks/.

CHAPTER 27

1. Verdon, Joan. "Barbie Movie Boosted Mattel's Sales, but Investors Held Their Applause." *Forbes*, October 27, 2023. https://www.forbes.com/sites/joanverdon/2023/10/25/barbie-movie-boosted-mattels-sales-but-investors-held-their-applause/?sh=640c9c8c1bd4.

CHAPTER 28

1. "Edelman Trust Barometer Special Report: In Brands We Trust?" Edelman. Accessed May 15, 2024. https://www.edelman.com/research/trust-barometer-special-report-in-brands-we-trust.

2. Kaminsky, Kathryn, Kathy Neiland, and Wes Bricker. "Trust Survey: Key Findings and Lessons for Business Executives." Harvard Law School Forum on Corporate Governance, April 30, 2023. https://corpgov.law.harvard.edu/2023/04/30/. trust-survey-key-findings-and-lessons-for-business-executives/.

3. "Trust Barometer Special Report: Brand Trust in 2020." Edelman. Accessed May 15, 2024. https://www.edelman.com/research/ brand-trust-2020.

4. "Newswire: Consumer Trust in Online, Social and Mobile Advertising Grows." Nielsen, July 21, 2022. https://www.nielsen.com/insights/2012/ consumer-trust-in-online-social-and-mobile-advertising-grows/.

5. Afshar, Vala. "New Research Uncovers Big Shifts in Customer Expectations and Trust." Salesforce, November 25, 2020. https://www. salesforce.com/blog/digital-customers-research-blog/.

6. "Buyer Enablement | Sales Insights | Gartner.Com." Gartner. Accessed May 16, 2024. https://www.gartner.com/en/sales/insights/buyer-enablement#:~:text=In%20a%20survey%20of%20more,quality%20 information%20available%20to%20buyers.

CHAPTER 29

1. Martech, Author. "Customer Lifetime Value: What It Is and Why It Matters." Wharton Online, December 19, 2022. https://online.wharton. upenn.edu/blog/why-customer-lifetime-value-matters/.

2. Duffy, James. "Ultimate Customer Loyalty Statistics 2022." More Than Accountants, February 25, 2022. https://www.morethanaccountants. co.uk/ultimate-customer-loyalty-statistics-2019/#Loyalty_Winners.

CHAPTER 30

1. "How Can Social Media Listening Increase Customer Advocacy." Serendipit Consulting—Brand Marketing and PR Company, February 23, 2023. https://serendipitconsulting.com/ how-can-social-media-listening-increase-customer-advocacy.

2. "HubSpot Reaches 100,000 Customers and $1 Billion in Revenue." CX Today. Accessed July 2, 2024. https://www.cxtoday.com/crm/ hubspot-reaches-100000-customers-and-1-billion-in-revenue/.

3. "Business Performance." Subaru Corporation. Accessed May 15, 2024. https://www.subaru.co.jp/en/ir/individualinvestors/performance.html.

4. "Yeti Holdings Revenue 2016–2024: Yeti." Macrotrends. Accessed May 15, 2024. https://www.macrotrends.net/stocks/charts/YETI/yeti-holdings/ revenue.

5. Bryan, Hannah. "Trader Joe's Secret to Success." Leaders.com, March 18, 2023. https://leaders.com/news/growth/trader-joes-secret-to-success/.

6. "Annual Report 2023." JetBlue. Accessed July 2, 2024. https://s202.q4cdn. com/853609783/files/doc_financials/2024/ar/JBLU023_JetBlue_2023-Annual-Report_Web.pdf.

7. Warby Parker Fourth Quarter and Full Year 2023 Results—Warby Parker. Accessed May 16, 2024. https://investors.warbyparker.com/news/news-details/2024/Warby-Parker-Announces-First-Quarter-2024-Results/default.aspx.

8. Tighe, D. "Nike: Gross Profit Worldwide 2023." Statista, August 15, 2023. https://www.statista.com/statistics/1002883/gross-profit-of-nike-worldwide/.

CHAPTER 31

1. "Blockbusted: A Netflix Knock-Out, Bad Metaphors on the Path to the Movie Monster's Bankruptcy." Accessed May 16, 2024. https://www.fastcompany.com/1685375/blockbusted-netflix-knock-out-bad-metaphors-path-movie-monsters-bankruptcy.

2. Siegler, MG. "Snoozing and Losing: A Blockbuster Failure." TechCrunch, May 5, 2024. https://techcrunch.com/2011/04/06/make-it-a-blockbuster-night/.

CHAPTER 32

1. "Salesforce Develops the Technology, the Partnerships, and the Communities That Help Companies Connect with Customers." Salesforce. Accessed May 15, 2024. https://www.salesforce.com/company/our-story/.

2. "Successful Brand Strategy Example (Old Spice Repositioning)." Brand Master Academy, April 6, 2024. https://brandmasteracademy.com/brand-strategy-example/.

3. Note: Stats collected in 2023. "How Netflix Survived the Streaming Wars to Stay the Subscription Video King." *Los Angeles Times*, March 6, 2024. https://www.latimes.com/entertainment-arts/business/story/2024-03-06/how-netflix-held-onto-its-crown-as-king-of-streaming.

4. "Crisis Communication Strategies." University of Oklahoma. Accessed May 15, 2024. https://www.ou.edu/deptcomm/dodjcc/groups/02C2/Johnson%20&%20Johnson.htm.

5. Ibid.

CONCLUSION

1. Arenas, Guillermo. "The Day Michael Jordan's Mother Changed Nike's History Forever: 'Even If You Don't Like It, You're Going to Listen to Them.'" EL PAÍS English, April 7, 2023. https://english.elpais.com/culture/2023-04-07/the-day-michael-jordans-mother-changed-nikes-history-forever-even-if-you-dont-like-it-youre-going-to-listen-to-them.html.

2. Haden, Jeff. "The 45-Year-Old Internal Memo That Set the Stage for Nike to Become a $135 Billion Company." Accessed October 17, 2022. https://www.inc.com/jeff-haden/nike-internal-memo-company-culture.html.

3.   Orlandon, Howard. "The Making of Nike's Lordship in Digital Marketing." Medium, December 25, 2021. https://medium.com/@orlandonhoward/the-making-of-nikes-lordship-in-digital-marketing-a16c7671cd24.

ACKNOWLEDGMENTS

"Oh, the places you'll go! There is fun to be done!
There are points to be scored. There are games to be won!"
—DR. SEUSS, *OH, THE PLACES YOU'LL GO*

Thank you for buying this book and for being an Unrivaler! I am forever grateful to you for trusting me in your business growth journey. You are Unrivaled . . . **Giddy Up!**

As I'm writing these acknowledgments, I'm soaking in the feeling of doing something bold and audacious with people I love and admire. I keep pinching myself at how lucky I am. *Unrivaled* would not have been possible without the efforts of so many incredible people who helped me in so many ways.

I'd like to start by thanking my incredible husband and family. Family is everything to me, and I really feel like I won the lottery.

Gary Fleming, your unwavering partnership, love, and advice, along with countless meals, pep talks, glasses of wine, chocolate, and sanity breaks, helped me make the dream of writing this book a reality. *Je t'aime toujours.*

James Heath, Maddie Heath, J. J. Heath, Gabrielle Simon, Erik Simon, Dylan Fleming, Jackie Fleming, thank you for being uniquely you. Your love, encouragement, and inspiration at every step have meant the world to me. I am grateful every day for our "very modern family" and for my "Gigi status." And, of course, to Baxter—the best dog ever, who thinks he's a ten-pound lapdog—for the many reminders to take a break, go for a walk, roll in the grass, enjoy a belly rub, eat a treat, and have the zoomies.

To my parents, Mary and Bob Abair, for instilling the gifts of love, compassion, grit, and resiliency in me, and showing me that anything is possible. Lisa Vuona, my sister and "Dallface," thank you for always being there for me and providing endless encouragement and therapy sessions when I need them most. And to my Peanut (Lily Vuona) and Justin (Justin Robert Vuona), I'm lucky to be your auntie. To my Montreal family, Micheline and Hank Fleming, Kim Fleming and Pierre Côté, Amanda Kellock and Dean Fleming, I am incredibly grateful for each of you and your love and friendship at every step. *Bonjour pamplemousse!* And to Andrea Rendon, for sharing your motherly love, kindness, and commitment to our family for so many years while I built my career and the seedlings of this book, *muchas gracias*, Mini!

To my business partner, Lily Weitzman, you are Unrivaled! Thank you for being the yin to my yang and for taking this some-days-borderline-insane journey with me. Your smarts, energy, passion, creativity, "flow," and abundance mindset make me and the world better. And to Rob and Ben Leaton, thank you for understanding the many long nights and countless hours and giving Lily and I the wings to create Unrivaled!

None of this would be possible without my Unrivaled Book Team: Gary Fleming for keeping things a well-oiled machine. Lily Weitzman for setting deadlines and making them happen like a boss. Risa Kent for your incredible design talent, eagle eye, and ability to channel what I'm thinking, bring ideas to life, and turn small details into big differences. Marji Ross for your Unrivaled manuscript coaching, advice, and partnership that made this book better and "birthed the baby!" Julie Stewart for your editorial mastery and commitment. Naren Aryal, Jenna Scafuri, and the entire Amplify Publishing Group team, for believing in me and *Unrivaled* and launching this book out into the world. ***Giddy Up!***

My A Team and inner circle of incredible thought-partners, subject matter experts, friends, and colleagues, thank you for your contributions to *Unrivaled*. Notably, Katherine Otway, for your endless inspiration, many whiteboard sessions, and strategic workshops that made the framework even better. Nathan Burke, for being the epitome of leading with brand and inspiring me to bang the drum and write the book. John Matos, for your advice, friendship, candor, and unwavering support during this writing process and helping me make the final manuscript a reality. Jerry Patterson for giving me my first leadership role, letting me find my wings (and boss you around!), and for showing me what great leadership looks like—thank you, my friend, for setting the bar high as I reach for this dream. Deepali Kakar, for your "quiet mastery" and bold support of me writing this book—forever grateful for you and our friendship. Mona Patel, for meeting me in a coffee shop in NYC where I first said the words out loud: "I'm writing a book!" and for the countless conversations author-to-author along this journey. And to the people and teams I had the honor to lead and work alongside at so many different steps along the way, I learned something from each of you. The many stories in this book were inspired by your dedication, passion, and expertise. You are Unrivaled!

To my incredible clients, thank you for your drive, passion, open-mindedness, and partnership. It is an honor to build an Unrivaled company alongside each of you! To all the brands I mention in the book, thanks for teaching us important lessons and keeping us in a growth mindset.

To my dear friends, near and far—people I have had the good fortune to meet at so many different points in my life: childhood-life, high school-life, college-life, work-life, mom-life, city-life, country-life, entrepreneur-life, just-life—you know who you are. It would fill many pages to capture every name. I feel so incredibly lucky that my cup runs over with people who are in my corner, there to pick me up when I'm down, and who love me unconditionally. Thank you for your friendship and support—my heart is full. *Carpe diem!*

To the many writers and authors who shared stories with me, provided advice, and helped me see the light at the end of the tunnel, thank you!

To my LinkedIn "family"—all of you who support my journey, embrace "the Giddy Up!", jump into the comments, share my posts, and contribute to our awesome community. You are Unrivaled!

And, finally, in the words of Snoop Dogg, during his 2018 speech as he received his long-awaited star on the Hollywood Walk of Fame:

"I want to thank me. I want to thank me for believing in me. I want to thank me for doing all this hard work. I want to thank me for having no days off. I want to thank me for never quitting. I want to thank me for always being a giver and trying to give more than I receive. I want to thank me for trying to do more right than wrong. I want to thank me for just being me at all times."*

Giddy Up!

---

* *Nappy Boy Radio with T-Pain* https://www.youtube.com/watch?v=T9X3YkgZRGo

ABOUT THE AUTHOR

Michelle Heath's sought-after business advice is the culmination of three decades under the hood of hundreds of businesses. Whether it's early-stage start-ups or Fortune 500 companies, Michelle has discovered what makes one business successful while another can't get past "go." Her extraordinary track record includes tenure as a brand, marketing, and customer experience executive for household brands, including Fidelity Investments, J.P. Morgan, and E*TRADE Financial. Michelle jumped off the corporate ladder to build start-ups, and in 2013, she founded Growth Street and pioneered the fractional growth leadership category. Using her proprietary Unrivaled Growth Framework™, she sets her clients up for go-to-market success, resulting in more than $100 billion in revenue growth.

Michelle is a top LinkedIn voice and frequent podcast guest. She is a board member and advisor for a variety of companies and shares her expertise with universities, start-up accelerators, and entrepreneurship programs. Michelle is a graduate of Boston University Questrom School of Business and lives in Boston, Massachusetts, with her family and beloved dog, Baxter the Boxer.